GROW YOUR ROOTS ANYWHERE, ANYTIME

GROW YOUR ROOTS ANYWHERE, ANYTIME

*Moving? New in town?
Two relocation specialists present
their painless program that
works for every uprooted family.*

**By Dr. Ronald J. Raymond, Jr.
and Dr. Stephen V. Eliot**

with Marilyn Mercer

A PETER H. WYDEN BOOK
Peter H. Wyden, Inc., Publisher
RAWSON, WADE PUBLISHERS, INC.

FIRST EDITION

Library of Congress Cataloging in Publication Data

Raymond, Ronald J
     Grow your roots anywhere, anytime.

     Bibliography: p.
     1. Employees, Relocation of—United States—Psychological aspects. I. Eliot, Stephen V., joint author. II. Mercer, Marilyn, joint author. III. Title.
HF5549.5.R47R39   648'.9'019   80-51703
ISBN 0-89256-152-1

ACKNOWLEDGMENTS

This book comes out of the wealth of experience that people across the country shared when they offered to talk to us, answer questionnaries, and write to us, and from the lives of thousands of transferees we have counseled. The accounts of these experiences are all from real people and are based on real situations. Only names were changed to safeguard privacy. So our picture of relocation problems and solutions is not drawn from an ivory tower or from the treatment of *patients.* It comes from participants. They tell it "like it is." So do we.

The best part of gathering data for this book has been the wonderful experiences we have had with so many transferees and the unending cooperation they gave us. To all we are deeply indebted and grateful.

Ronald J. Raymond, Jr., Ph.D., ABPP
Stephen V. Eliot, Ph.D.

TABLE OF CONTENTS

Appendices

Bibliography

GROW YOUR ROOTS
ANYWHERE, ANYTIME

THE UPROOTED AMERICANS

America, as everybody knows, is the land of the upwardly mobile. We've always put the emphasis on the word *upwardly*. It's time to take a closer look at the word *mobile* because the U. S. Bureau of the Census says that an almost incredible 40 million Americans—20 percent of the population—change their place of residence every year. Some are first-time movers, leaving the parental nest for college, marriage, or their own apartment. Some are last-time movers— retired people packing up their pensions and their memories to seek the good life in a warm climate. Many don't move very far—maybe across town to a bigger and better (or smaller and cheaper) house or apartment. Others go halfway across the continent, sometimes only because, for unaccountable reasons, the grass looks greener out there beyond familiar territory.

This book is for all of them, the uprooted. Its self-help strategies, tactics and tips, all carefully tested by us and by our individual and corporate clients, are tailored to help you (whether you're single, married or divorced) at all turns of the moving trail: before the first move you ever make on your own; or before any new move, no matter how often you've already relocated; or when you first start trying to get reestablished in a new environment; or at any time after you move but still find yourself feeling more or less uprooted.

Among our uprooted, one group is more clearly identifiable. These are the families who move not because they have to and not because they necessarily want to but because the breadwinner of the family is being transferred ("relocated") by "the company." Relocation has become a big industry, and its authorities estimate that corporations transfer some 300,000 people annually. That doesn't include their families. Nor does it include people in the academic or professional worlds.

These 300,000 are the corporate uprooted, and their tribe is increasing constantly. They also tend to be repeaters. Among this group, two out of every five households move every three years, and one out of five actually moves *annually*, according to Welcome Wagon International, and they should know.

HITCHING THE COVERED WAGON

Social analysts will tell you that we've always been a mobile society and cite the pioneers who settled the West. Today's movers and shakers couldn't be more different.

The nineteenth century pioneers were either drifters or homesteaders. The homebodies packed their belongings into covered wagons and headed west, usually as part of a wagon train. On the journey, these families frequently formed cohesive groups and firm friendships. They camped together, hunted together and fought off hostile Indians together. And that was only the beginning of a great and perfectly natural togetherness.

Once they reached their particular allotment of the promised land, the newcomers settled in, felling trees to build shelter, plowing stubborn virgin soil to put in crops. They endured the hardships of freezing winters, parched rainless summers, and plain backbreaking work. If the Lord was willing, the creek didn't rise, and they weren't wiped out by Indians, they founded a community. And there they stayed, no longer uprooted but newly rooted.

GO WEST . . . AND EAST . . . AND . . .

To the present day transferee, this is the stuff of western movies. He (or, increasingly, she) is not setting out to settle anything except perhaps the delicate matter of where he* stands in the hierarchy of his company. Horace Greeley's words "Go West, young man, go West" have long lost their inspirational clout. The new mobile American packs his goods into a moving van, his family into a station wagon and heads west or east or north or south for a promised land (well, the company promised he'd like it, didn't it?) already over-populated by people he doesn't know and isn't at all sure he'll like. And he moves with the almost certain knowledge that he or she will be asked by the company to move again in two or three years, in some cases back where he came from.

In today's large, very large, and national, if not inter-national, companies or conglomerates, the typical transferee is part of middle management. He is usually sent out to func-tion within an established installation. The move may mean a promotion or it may be lateral, for the convenience of the company. Or it may be a group move in which an entire division of a company is relocated. It is less often regarded (by the employee, at least) as an honor, more often as a duty. And in many cases he or she (more than 5 percent of trans-

---

* No, we're not sexists. We're just vexed by the gender rule limitations of the grammarians. Throughout this book "he" refers to both sexes inter-changeably.

ferees are women) will be asked not only to move again but again and again.

THERE'S ORGANIZED HELP

Today his company automatically assumes his moving expenses, and the relocation industry bustles to fill his needs. The most obvious need is the locating, buying and selling of homes, and over a dozen large companies and many smaller ones now offer this service to industry on highly sophisticated terms. Working under contract with employers, these firms are prepared to offer a selection of available houses to the transferred employee based on his needs, income and personal preference; undertake the shipping of goods; and, in a few cases; purchase the houses vacated by transferees for resale later through their own or other real estate agents. At least 30 percent of all corporate moves are handled by such companies. A transferring family need only select the new house in the new location; announce their date of departure; and leave everything else, from the financing of the new home and disposal of the old one to packing and transporting household goods, to the professional relocation experts.

To orient the uprooted in the new community and to help them meet people there's Welcome Wagon International of Memphis, Tennessee, serving some 3,000 communities, and New Neighbors League with headquarters in Dayton, Ohio, serving eleven states. Welcome Wagon depends on commissions from local merchants whose goods and services they call to the attention of newcomers; New Neighbors depends on membership dues. Both essentially fill the same function: through personal visits, club meetings and planned activities, they offer new families in town a chance to get their social bearings. In addition, countless locally organized newcomers clubs without formal affiliation serve the same purpose.

HOW OFTEN CAN YOU MOVE?

For more and more of today's transferees, a nice new house perhaps with financing eased by the company and an invitation to a jolly newcomer's party is just for starters. This is especially true if the transferred family has moved more than twice (and among the corporate uprooted most couples have moved more than twice while they're still in their twenties).

These services and organizations like the Employee Relocation Council are essential to the newly mobile society. Where would we be without them? But there's a deeper problem that the helping services don't attack directly, and this is where we have been of help to these families and can also be of help to you in this book. That deeper, more personal problem is the subtle and sometimes not so subtle psychological jarring that repeated relocations will trigger in a relocating individual and his or her family.

How many times can we successfully tear up our roots and transplant them again? It can be done, successfully and rewardingly, more often than you may think. It does require some specialized guidance, and we've acquired the experience to offer this support to you here and now.

ARE YOU FEELING LIKE A PAWN?

Constant moving can take a toll on the prime mover in the family; more often than not, after several moves he begins to feel like a pawn in a giant corporate chess game.

It takes its toll on his dependent family, too. Even more so when family members are independent or reaching for independence—the wife with a job of her own, the teen-agers with school ties and career plans that are disrupted by a move.

These factors complicate relocations so that corporations are understandably worried about losing valuable people. Indeed, sometimes they *are* losing them. More and more family heads are refusing to move. A need has arisen for professionals who help families make the move—not physically but emotionally. That is the role of our company, Transition, Inc.

Get ready to meet some interesting people with interesting problems in these pages! Like Phil Green, who didn't realize that after twenty years with his company he really wanted to get off (not up) the corporate ladder; John Sinter, who almost cheated himself out of an exciting, constructive move by making negative (and wrong) assumptions about his new environment; and Lilly Wilson, who, though she was bright and competent, denied that her family relocation was responsible for one of her children's sudden physical problems.

Neither of us set out to make a career of counseling transferees. Ten year ago, although between us we had relocated a total of sixteen times, we were not fully aware of the need for this service. But as chance would have it, both of us (first Ron, then Steve) signed on as staff psychologists at the prestigious Silver Hill Foundation in Connecticut.

We weren't sure at the time what we would find there. Silver Hill maintained the highest professional standards. Most of the patients come from the corporate world. In our long sessions with these troubled individuals a common denominator emerged. Most of them came to Silver Hill to be treated for a variety of psychiatrically recognized problems (severe anxiety, various forms of depression, borderline schizophrenia or alcoholism) and they had one life stress in common. Most of them, because of their own or their spouses' professions, led mobile, rootless lives.

In these severe cases, other (more severe) problems were involved, but for the majority the stress of constant moving, added to other sources of stress, helped push them to the point where hospitalization became necessary. The most interesting part of this was that rarely did any of these people make the connection between their relocations and their experience of stress and their symptoms. Never having been given the chance to consider some of their reactions to their relocation trauma as normal to the situation, they lumped *all* their problems together, which caused them to become exaggerated, so they called themselves "sick." As we said before, relocation can in no way be labeled as the primary cause of emotional difficulty; but it was exciting to see the change when at least that aspect of a person's difficulties was understood and treated.

We asked ourselves: what happens to ordinary husbands, wives and children who relocate regularly at company request and seem to suffer no apparent emotional damage?

EVERYBODY WANTS TO TALK ABOUT IT

We began investigating, querying couple after couple who had moved frequently. To our surprise the task of gathering information was not nearly as difficult as we first anticipated. People readily volunteered and seemed eager to tell their relocation stories. This incredible willingness (and need) to relate their transfer experiences quickly validated for us the magnitude of the problem and the need for professional attention. And we learned that for virtually all relocating families, some degree of hidden emotional stresses is as inevitable as the arrival of the moving van.

Our research was confirmed by articles in newspapers, magazines and other publications, detailing the loneliness of the long-distance mover and the adjustment difficulties of his family, but offering no solutions to this serious problem. We were surprised by the light treatment in most of the articles. Everybody seemed to be taking superficial pot shots at dealing with the topic. In a busines journal there would be no mention of sociological or psychological publications. These other disciplines were guilty of the same isolated treatment of the subject. Most important, still no solutions were offered; *no one* was attempting to help relocating families to find and use the positive aspects of the experience.

There *is* a solution. Working with thousands of transferees, we learned that the problems can be dealt with once the people involved understand and acknowledge the true source of their anxieties. This book details our method of helping these families, step by step, so you can apply it to yourself and your family.

YOU CAN GAIN IN MANY WAYS

We also learned that there is more to relocation counseling than minimizing the stresses of moving. The moving experience *can* be turned into a positive experience, not only to achieve job advancement for the breadwinner but personal growth and enrichment for all the family.

First, a move gives the entire family a common goal. The family that truly shares the experience and discusses feelings openly frequently feels closer and develops better relationships within the family group. The family that's constantly on the move becomes familiar not only with one way of life but many. Nobody can call mobile people provincial. They can hang on to old friends while making new ones. They become seasoned travelers at company expense. The child who learned in his formative years to adjust to new schools, new cities, and different kinds of people will have far fewer problems when he goes to college than a classmate leaving home for the first time. And the couple who has relocated successfully many times should have little difficulty finding and settling in) the perfect retirement spot.

In an increasingly fluid world, the transferees are new

pioneers, after all, because they're getting invaluable experience at enjoying what's becoming a more and more normal and certainly no longer exceptional lifestyle.

THE TRANSFER NEUROSIS

"What's the big deal about moving? People do it all the time." We hear this often—from people who don't move very often if at all.

To most stay-at-homes, their peripatetic neighbors lead exciting lives indeed. There's open envy in their voices when neighbors relay the news that Linda and Tom are moving to Texas ("She showed me pictures of the house—it has an *atrium.*"); or that Sam and Martha are heading for the bright lights of Chicago; or best of all, Tess and Pete are being transferred overseas and will have their own villa and servants.

That's how it looks from the neighbors' perspective. But to Linda and Tom, Sam and Martha, and even Tess and Pete, newly of the international set, whether the destination is Buenos Aires or Butte, Montana, it mostly means one more round of packing and unpacking, finding new doctors and dentists, finding new schools, finding new friends.

To the community at large, the couple tapped for transfer puts its best face forward, extolling the advantages of the new location and showing off polaroids of the house with the atrium. To their close friends they're apt to complain a little (or even a lot) about the endless practical problems a move entails, to say nothing of the difficulty of getting mortgage money.

What they don't tell friends about, usually because they don't fully comprehend it themselves, is the constellation of emotional stresses that repeated relocations trigger within the family unit—strains which, if unacknowledged and not dealt with, can eventually cause the family to fall apart like a pylon on an unchecked DC 10.

These stresses and strains are characteristic and predictable, so much so that all together we call them the *transfer neurosis*.

WHEN ANXIETIES RUB OFF
ON MORE ANXIETIES

Technically, the syndrome is not really a neurosis. Neuroses are internally caused. In relocation, the cause or causes are external, yet they can produce neurotic symptoms in an otherwise well functioning person. It can almost be compared to battle fatigue. Alvin Toffler, discussing our newly mobile society in *Future Shock*, writes: "Millions sense the pathology that pervades the air, but fail to understand its roots."

Its roots are buried in the complex of anxieties, traumas, fears and threats that accompany the act of moving from one place to another. All of them are recognized by psychologists, and are relatively easy for most people to deal with on their own when these problems pop up one at a time. But the constantly moving family (or any individual member) may suffer from any combination of these anxieties at one time or, most often, all of them at once.

That's not all. The anxieties, fears and traumas of one family member inevitably rub off on the anxieties, fears and traumas of other family members, which creates a new set of problems, often for the entire group.

Without insight, the more you move, the worse it can get.

We call this "cumulative relocation fatigue," but putting a name on it doesn't solve the problem.

What does? For starters, analyzing the component parts does.

HOW'S YOUR SEPARATION ANXIETY?

This catchall term accounts for many of the emotional traumas of moving.

All living creatures experience anxiety when they're separated from loving and protective figures in their lives. When a baby duck loses sight of its mother, it panics, runs about frantically and emits little squawks (the duck distress signal) until the mother returns. The human toddler, left by his mother in a day care center or with a sitter, may break into screams of infant protest. The protesting child is upset not only because he feels abandoned, but because he simultaneously fears that disaster will befall the departed parent.

We do not normally hear duck squawks or infant screams from unhappy transferred businessmen and their families. But a similar emotional mechanism is at work.

And it's at work in a number of ways. First, there's separation within the family. In a typical transfer, the husband may depart for the new location weeks or even months ahead of the rest of the family. The left-behind wife commonly experiences some degree of separation anxiety.

"We'd only been married two months," said Rachel Karlson, "when Al got transferred to Cleveland. He had to leave right away, of course, and here I was, a new wife with a new apartment, suddenly alone. I'd just gotten used to living away from my parents. I felt like I'd been widowed before I got used to being married."

It happens with older wives, too. "I thought I had moving down pat," said Sally Morrison. "But when Herb changed companies, it was a new ball game. He had to go to L.A. without me for four months, and I really panicked.

"Here I was at forty-two, suddenly husbandless and not knowing what awaited me in the new situation. I mean, I wasn't entirely *for* Herb changing companies. Was the new job going to work out? Tim and Amy, my teen-agers, chose that time to inform me that I could move to Los Angeles if I wanted to, but *they* were staying in Philadelphia. Oh, *great*! And on top of that, I'm now ashamed to say, I began worrying that Herb had or would find a new woman."

There are umpteen variations on the same theme. You can probably supply your own.

Small children, suddenly deprived of their father, are apt to feel confused, rejected, bereaved, abandoned or any combination thereof. Little ones are (usually) easily comforted. If one parent is away, the other is still there. The eight-year-old who asks "Why did Daddy go away?" is satisfied with "Daddy went away because he has a wonderful new job and in a little while we're all going to join him and have a lovely new house and . . ." (Expert mothers here fill in whatever will please their particular child.)

THE TEEN-AGERS GO ON STRIKE

With teen-agers, it isn't so simple. Sally Morrison's Tim and Amy are fairly typical. They've developed adult defense mechanisms, and their reaction to an unwanted move is bravado: "Hell no, we won't go!"

Meanwhile, Daddy, the focal point of all this family turmoil, is having his own separation anxiety problems. His side of it, if he's typical of the many husbands we've counseled in these situations, goes something like this.

"The new job was a terrific opportunity for me and for all of us. Sally didn't entirely realize (maybe I didn't really tell her) that I had about gone the course with the company, so going in as West Coast sales manager with the chief competitor was a terrific break. Yes, I know I had to leave the family alone for a while. Yes, I know they were unhappy about it, and I feel plenty guilty about that. But if Sally thinks I was living it up in L.A. with parties and women every night, I wasn't. I was living in a motel room, and that can get lonely.

"I feel helpless about Tim and Amy. When they were little kids, they didn't mind moving. Why can't they understand now?"

Sometimes it works the other way, and the family adjusts better to separation than the relocated father.

When Andy Beck was transferred from East Hartford to Dallas, he had to spend two months in the new location before his family could join him.

"I was miserable," he recalls. "In the past, when I got back from short business trips, everyone threw their arms around me and told me how much they missed me. I really felt needed, and maybe a little guilty about being away for a whole week.

"In Dallas, I began to think maybe I wasn't. After the first two weeks, they all adjusted just fine to my absence.

"The last time I called, my wife was at a meeting, my teen-age daughter was at a party, and my son, who answered the phone, couldn't talk because he was watching a baseball game on TV with a friend."

It wasn't really that the family didn't miss him. It was simply that they had each other and their friends, and he was alone and experiencing separation anxiety more acutely than they were.

HANDLING SEPARATION FROM THE FAMILY

Few adults today will admit to missing their own parents. It's understandable. In rural America, a young man was supposed to strike out on his own by the time he reached the age of eighteen. Those who didn't were regarded as somehow suspect. "Tied to momma's apron strings" was the descriptive phrase. His bride, being a woman and therefore "frail," was allowed to miss her mother for perhaps a year. But after the first child, she was expected to shape up.

Freudian and post-Freudian psychiatrists made matters worse. Being tied to mother's apron strings is a relatively mild accusation compared to the psychosexual implications of a full-fledged Oedipus complex. The individual who won't leave the parental nest (or is otherwise totally dependent on mom and dad) *is* in trouble, but that's not the kind of trouble we're discussing.

First of all, it's unfashionable to acknowledge that adults need their parents in any way; in fact, parents are invaluable for support that can't quite be replaced by companions and friends, and when we're separated from them, at any age, we feel an emotional wrench.

We're talking about a secondary form of separation anxiety, the kind that's commonly felt by couples who are (geographically) far away from their own parents. This can develop into a burdensome sense of guilt, especially if parents are ailing or elderly.

"I'm really upset about this move," Alice Mayberry told us. "Ever since Dad had his heart attack, I feel one of us should be home. Mom isn't getting any younger, and my sister Frances has just moved to the West Coast."

Sometimes guilt translates into anger, which can be even more destructive. Harry Adams' story is familiar: "My mother, God bless her, is driving me up the wall! She wanted me to take this job, you understand; she wants me to be successful so she can brag to the neighbors. Okay, so it means I have to live half a continent away from her. Now she's complaining—says I neglect her. What am I supposed to do? Call home every night?"

Children of mobile families miss grandparents acutely, if, that is, they have grown to know them. Some, of course, don't, such as seven-year-old Mike who asked his mother why he didn't have a grandma like the other kids.

"But you do," said his mother. "Don't you remember? Nana Parker—you met her at Aunt Lucy's when we visited there for Christmas."

"Was that my grandma?" said Mike. "I thought she was the lady from next door."

MEET YOUR TERRITORIAL IMPERATIVE

Leaving any particular community should not be overly traumatic, or so we like to believe. Especially when the move is from, let's say, a dull small town to an exciting big city. But ironically enough, it often causes much pain. There's a reason. All animals have an instinctive need to claim their turf. It's called the *territorial imperative*. For the human animal this instinct is more complicated. His turf becomes part of his identity, and that's hard to part with.

"I know I should appreciate being transferred from West Plainville to New York," said the wife of a plant manager, who recently made vice-president. "Charlie is making a lot more money, we have a beautiful home in Connecticut, the schools are good here, the people couldn't be nicer—but I miss West Plainville. We lived there for fifteen years. It's home."

Charlie, a vigorous, urbane man of forty-seven, is in complete accord. "I certainly appreciate being promoted," he said. "Of course I like the new house, the good schools. The kids like it here a lot. But I'm like Rita—I miss West Plainville. Life was nice and low-key there. It took me ten minutes to drive to the plant. Here, it takes over an hour to drive to New York, even in my nice new sports car." He laughed.

"I sound like some character out of the movies, an old country guy moved to the big city. I'm not. I was born in New York and I sure can't ride a horse. One of the problems about this part of Connecticut is that I may have to learn! I guess I'm just plain homesick.

"Believe me, I've been thinking about it. When I'm fifty-five, I'm going to take early retirement, cash in my stock options and Rita and I are going back to West Plainville. I know I can't go back to running the plant, but I'll have enough to do *something*. Maybe I'll open a general store."

Charlie and Rita are among the more fortunate ones. Phil and Margie Reuter, who were transferred from the New York area to a town much like West Plainville, fared worse, much worse.

"I'm quitting," Phil told us. "I don't know what I'm going to do next, but Margie just can't take this. She's never been away from the East Coast before—we lived in New York, Boston and New Jersey before this—and suddenly being dumped in this hick town is just too much. I guess she's tired—she's had a lot of hassles moving with three young kids—but this time I think she's going to crack up. I'd send her to a psychiatrist, except there isn't one within 100 miles."

A HOUSE IS NOT A HOME

For many people, leaving a house is harder than leaving a community. You don't have to be a psychologist to figure this out. Edgar A. Guest, rural America's favorite old poet, knew all about it. "It takes a heap o' living in a house to make it home," Mr. Guest observed and, trite as it sounds to lovers of more mature literature, Mr. Guest was right on target. For those who have put a "heap o' living" in a house, leaving it can be deeply traumatic.

The shelves a man puts up, the kitchen a woman designs, the garden they plant together are not any old shelves, kitchens or gardens. None may make *House Beautiful*, but to that couple they're landmarks of their lives. They turned a house into a home.

Hear Charlie Schacter: "I was perfectly willing to transfer from Jersey to Illinois. The thing that stuck in my craw was leaving the family room that Lois and I made in the basement. When we first moved into the Springfield house, the basement was a mess. Dirty, dusty, with nothing but a furnace. The former family had used it as a storage place. Lois and I cleaned it up, put in flooring, walls, furniture and turned it into a family and party room. We had some of our best times in that basement and so did the kids.

"Yes, we're moving into a new house with a finished basement, but it isn't the same. And don't tell me to find an old house and fix up the basement again. I've done all that. I don't want to do it again."

Lois, his wife, was more explicit. "The real estate agents always call the new houses they offer you 'homes.' They're not.

"You know what? We used to live in a home. It wasn't all that great, but it was where we lived. On the doorframe in the Springfield house are marks that show how tall Mark and Jennifer were when they three, six, nine, and ten. If a real estate agent can recreate *that*—okay, it's a new home."

Charlie and Lois were very explicit about what they missed. Others throw up generalized defenses.

"I couldn't care less what they move us into," Eleanor Parker told us. "I mean, really, a house is a house. I used to care about those things. When we started, we had a little apartment in New York. I used to love to fix it up—God knows, it needed fixing. Well, after Melissa was born, luckily Sid got sent to Boston. We had a big old house in Newton, and again, we had a fine time painting and plastering and turning an old barn into something fit to live in. Kenny and Ted were born in that house, and when we had to leave it the children had a screaming fit.

"Our next move was to a really lovely ranch house, with three bedrooms, and four baths, and now we have a colonial, with a gardener and, would you believe, a swimming pool? I don't have to do a thing. But it doesn't *feel* right."

Why then, with all these material blessings, was Eleanor

unhappy? Most people would envy her beautiful house, swimming pool and gardener. In further discussions with her, it became clear that owning a home was a small source of satisfaction to Eleanor compared to *creating* one, as she had done in the earlier years of her marriage.

In the course of sequential moves, Eleanor had her sand castles kicked out from under her so many times that she simply lost the ability to care or perhaps was afraid to care. And so she was left feeling empty, bored, restless and unsatisfied, having lost, without realizing it, what had been an important source of creative satisfaction.

FEAR OF THE UNKNOWN

Finally, there's the fear of the unknown, just because it is unknown. Most of the mobile families we have counseled feel this to a greater or lesser degree.

The breadwinner commonly has doubts and uncertainties about how the new job will really work out, no matter how great it sounds on paper. The whole family has doubts about how they, together and as individuals, will fit into the new setting. It's much like the last-minute panic felt by many travelers just before the ship sails or the plane takes off.

"It *always* happens to me," says a professional travel writer. "Usually while I'm packing. I suddenly decide I don't want to go and it's not too late to change my mind. But I always go anyway. I just tell myself, 'If you hate it, you can just turn around and go home.'"

The transferred family can't.

If you have felt (or are feeling) any or all the miseries described in this chapter, the key fact to remember is that you are not *alone*. Nor are you suffering from some form of mental aberration. Any reaction or behavior shared by large numbers of people in response to the same pressures is normal for those people. You need to isolate, acknowledge and understand these pressures and their consequences and find ways of coping with them before they build up and intensify to the point where they hold the potential or creating serious emotional problems. Unless you do, the *transfer neurosis* becomes a real neurosis.

IS THIS TRIP NECESSARY?

For some, it isn't. The employee who is highly regarded by the organization knows he can sometimes call his own shots. Jack Harris was Artex Corporation's star salesman. He was also a gifted manager. While his children were young, he moved willingly and often across the country and up the ladder, from salesman in Chicago to assistant sales manager in Houston to sales manager in Tampa to district sales manager in Boston.

There he called a halt. While his boys were in high school, he explained to his superiors, he wanted to stay put. The company agreed; it was better than losing Harris. When Josh and Anthony were safely in college, Jack and Eleanor were invited back to the home office in Chicago, an invitation that they accepted happily since it meant, for Eleanor, returning to her own hometown, and for Jack, a vice-presidency.

Jack Harris's story is encouraging but far from typical. The conventional wisdom is that the man who refuses to relocate seriously jeopardizes his future with the organization; and this conventional wisdom is usually right.

But it's far from being a cut-and-dried proposition that needs to be settled in an either/or way. The midde-management man who holds it as an article of faith that shaping up means shipping out may find out that he's wrong. And the company superstar may push his luck too far when he refuses to move again.

THERE MAY BE OPTIONS. And you owe it to yourself, your family, and your employer (nobody wants a payroll overburdened with malcontents) to explore possibilities in depth.

Even the option of changing jobs—voluntarily.

The first step, when you're faced with a transfer offer is to sit down by yourself and reevaluate your total career plan. By yourself, please. This is not the time to confer with family members, co-workers, or bosses. There is a Relocation Career Assessment on page 30 for your use. Work it out with pencil and paper. Don't worry, nobody is going to see this document but you.

Many people who started out five, ten or twenty years ago with a clear view of their career trajectory got bogged down somewhere in the middle. You may be a thirty-year-old man who set out at twenty-two to make a career for himself in business, and now, eight years later, realizes it isn't too late to enroll in law school. You may be a fifty-year-old woman who made it up the ladder despite your sex and find your ambition dwindling. What happens next, except to sit around and wait for the pension? Or you may be anybody of any age or any sex, who suspects it might be time for a change, but so far hasn't had any particular reason to face up to the situation.

An impending unwanted move provides a very good reason.

And it's possible that one of the reasons the move is unwanted is that down deep, you don't want to be with this particular company or in this particular line of work anyway. Lifetime career plans are always subject to change at your discretion. Don't be like the middle-aged, miserable dentist who said, speaking of himself at the age of eighteen, "I'm really sore at that kid who decided in college that I should spend my life filling teeth."

MAYBE IT'S TIME TO GET OUT?

The results of asking yourself this question may surprise you, as they did Phil Green.

"When I started out with ChemCo twenty years ago," he said, "I did it for money. They paid the highest starting salaries for executive trainees. My goal? Simple. $50,000 a year by forty-five. Well, I'm forty-four now, and the transfer they're offering pays $62,000. Right on target, considering inflation. But you know what? I'm turning it down. I've been plant manager here in Allensburg for seven years. I like it, I've done a good job, I've increased plant productivity by 40 percent and I get along fine with the union. Now they want me to come to New York as vice-president in charge of East Coast operations at a fancy salary, but I just don't want to go. If I can stay on here, I will. If I can't—well, there's another chemical company that's interested in my taking over one of their plants—and I know just how I could make it work for them."

After this discussion we asked Phil to complete the Relocation Career Assessment listing the importance of his goals on a scale from 1 (least) to 10 (highest)—with the following results.

Phil discovered that his feelings about not wanting the transfer and promotion made real sense because of the changes in his career goal system. When he told us how he felt he was relieved to see that his decision made sense. Frequently, people have the gut feeling that they do not want to transfer but they lack a way to understand why. So sometimes they feel their decision is based on whim, foolishness, immaturity or irrationality. When it's nothing of the kind.

PHIL GREEN'S RELOCATION CAREER ASSESSMENT

Part 1

Career Goals	Original	Today	Difference
Making a higher salary	8	8	0
Power and prestige	9	4	−5
Accomplishment	9	6	−3
Enjoying work on a day by day basis	5	10	+5
Having time to spend with family and friends	3	8	+5
Providing for family	10	10	0
Job security—retirement income	3	9	+6

PHIL GREEN'S RELOCATION CAREER ASSESSMENT

Part 2

Goals with +2 or −2 or greater difference	Why has the change occurred?
Power and prestige	I feel like I have shown myself that I can do it, and power no longer turns me on.
Accomplishment	The job I did for ChemCo couldn't have been done by many people, and again I feel like I proved myself.
Enjoy work on a day-by-day basis	I have to feel relaxed or I just don't think it's worth it.
Having time to spend with family and friends	This has become as important a source of gratification as work accomplishment was.
Job security—retirement income	I used to say I would never retire. Now I can see myself doing it and loving it, as long as I have income security.

PHIL GREEN'S RELOCATION CAREER ASSESSMENT
Part 3

Goals	Effect on goal by accepting transfer	Effect on goal by turning down transfer
Making a higher salary	Probably will far exceed original goal	May have to settle for slightly less
Power and prestige	More prestige	No change
Accomplishment	More at work	No change
Enjoying work on a day-by-day basis	Less; more pressure	More enjoyment
Having time to spend with family and friends	Less and have to make new ones at that	More time
Providing for family	More money	Maintain present living style
Job security, adequate retirement income	Can't be sure	Seems sure

This exercise can help you sort out and understand some of your feelings.

Phil's attitude about going with the other chemical company really did not fit with his chart. The increase for retirement income security, need for family time, and enjoying work along with the decrease in his need to start and see new projects to completion were not consistent with attacking the building of a new deparment and new labor relations.

His stance, almost in bravado, of being able to go elsewhere was really a defense. Phil felt that if he refused the move he would be forced to leave and was just covering his tracks so he'd always have an "out"—the feeling that he chose to quit. His perception of the corporation and his vice-president was that there would be no understanding of his turndown. He even considered leaving for the other company without discussing that the proposed move was the issue.

WHAT DO YOU REALLY THINK OF THE COMPANY?

The perception one has of his employer is critical. We encouraged Phil to question that perception. He did and wound up less sure of his ground. After much deliberation he did discuss with his vice-president why he did not want to accept the promotion and did want to continue doing the same job. He explained he felt fulfilled, productive and happy.

Phil still has a hard time believing that this was totally accepted by management. They took the occasion to praise him for the job he was doing. He was permitted to stay on in the same position and shortly afterwards got a modest raise.

Bob Connor's story is the flip side of Phil's. "I went with ChemCo," he said, "because they were a stable company, had a good insurance plan and excellent retirement benefits. I never expected to make a lot of money. I just wanted a steady job and security for myself and my family. I'm a good engineer and a good manager; I've taken promotions when they came my way, but never looked for them. I'm an assistant plant manager now and doing well—but, you know, it's boring.

"Now they want me to take over the Houston plant. The scuttlebutt is that it's a high risk job. The last guy couldn't make his quota and they fired him. But I'm still going to take it. Do you think I'm crazy?"

Not at all, we told him at the time, and it proved out. Bob took the Houston job, made a success of it, and now had a somewhat better pension to look forward to. Phil Green turned down the New York offer and is still with his company. He's not making $62,000, but he's happy in his work.

THE "FAMILY" THAT WASN'T THERE

Mary Hastings is forty-eight, divorced, and has a good job as a buyer in a branch of a New York department store. The crunch came when Mary was tapped for transfer and promotion to sportswear buyer in the New York City store. She didn't want to take it, and she didn't know why.

She took the Relocation Career Assessment and scored herself high on money, accomplishment, and providing for family.

"What family?" we asked her. "My son Ted," she said. "I put him through college myself. What do you think I've been working for?"

Gently, very gently, we reminded her that Ted was twenty-three now, fully educated and a grown, capable man on his own.

"You know, you're right," she said. "I'm not responsible for anyone but myself now."

Mary quit the store, opened her own dress shop in the community she had grown to love and is doing very nicely. Ted was delighted with her decision for reasons Mary probably wouldn't want to hear.

"As you can imagine," he said, "I heard a lot while I was growing up about the sacrifices Ma was making for me, and I felt guilty. I also felt she owned me, and when I heard she was going to New York for an even better job—well, I felt sort of helpless. But this is great. I've got my job and my problems, she's got her dress shop and her problems—and now we're really friends."

Bob, Phil and Mary all feel they made the right career choices. They're happy now with their work and with themselves.

An honest relocation job evaluation can do the same for you, especially at mid career. Use the Relocation Career Assessment to help you spell out for yourself: (1) reasons to stay with the company or consider a change; (2) how relocation will affect your present career and life goals.

Rate the importance of your career goals from 1 (least) to 10 (highest) for each goal as you viewed it in the beginning of your career and as you see it today. Calculate the change in importance for each goal and place the increase or reduction in the difference column below.

RELOCATION CAREER ASSESSMENT

Part 1

Career Goals	Original Goals	Today	Difference (+ or −)
Making a high salary			
Power and prestige			
Assomplishment: seeing a project through to its end			
Enjoying work on a day-by-day basis			
Having time to spend with family and friends			
Providing for family			
Job security— retirement income			

P.S. There's no need to add up any figures.

Take each goal which has changed by two or more points and list it in the first column below. In the adjoining column describe your understanding of why the change has occurred in the importance that you place on that goal.

RELOCATION CAREER ASSESSMENT

Part 2

List goals with +2 or −2 or greater difference	*Why has the change occurred?*
____________________	____________________
____________________	____________________
____________________	____________________
____________________	____________________
____________________	____________________
____________________	____________________
____________________	____________________

RELOCATION CAREER ASSESSMENT

Part 3

Write the effect that accepting or rejecting your job transfer would have on each goal listed.

Goals	*Effect on goal by accepting transfer*	*Effect on goal by turning down transfer*
Making a high salary		
Power and prestige		
Accomplishment: seeing a project through to its end		
Enjoying work on a day-by-day basis		
Having time to spend with family and friends		
Providing for family		
Job security— retirement income		

A second high priority factor needs to be weighed in your decision about whether this trip is necessary. What are your personal values? What's truly important to you and how is all this affected when you change *communities?*

We all live by very personal standards that we regard as important and that make up our total life style. The seventies brought a gradual change in priorities so that style of life and the pursuit of comfort and leisure time have become as important as work, at least for most people.

WHAT'S IMPORTANT TO YOU AND WHY?

We advise people to list and look carefully at whatever they regard as important outside their jobs. That's the easier part of this inquiry. People usually can pick out what's important to them. Often though, they do not take the time to analyze why, or what it is about a particular activity or situation that is especially meaningful. It's very useful for you to do this analysis and then examine how these values are affected by your accepting or refusing a transfer to a new location.

Everyone has a private set of things they value in life, but the way John Sinter filled out the Relocation Life Style Value Exercise will give you an idea of the process and how you can apply it to yourself.

John did not come up with anything startling to himself, but as he reviewed the exercise with his wife, who by the way also filled out the exercise with her own values, he began to see that he was placing too much emphasis on the way he saw the short term aspects.

This is one of the major errors people often make in assessing a move. It's difficult for them to see beyond the first few days. We have repeatedly had people describe the image of themselves in their new community-to-be, and most were still in the unpacking and very unsettled phase. Although difficult to do, you must try to picture yourself in the new location at least three months after moving in.

JOHN SINTER'S VALUE EXERCISE

Part 1

List 6 to 10 things of importance to you	What about these are meaningful to you?
1. My family's happiness	If my family is happy I feel I'm doing my job in life.
2. Having a few close friends	I need to feel I have people I can rely on and talk to if I have a major problem.
3. My church affiliation	I value my religion and feel it is essential to my security.
4. My woodworking hobby	A release of tension.
5. My parents' opinion of how I'm making it	It makes me feel I'm pleasing them.
6. Having a nice home and good car	I feel successful.

John really has no idea how "happy" his family will be, either where he is or in a new location, two years from now. This applies to most of us, yet we readily make assumptions about it all the time. It's easy to predict unhappiness because

Part 2

List 6 to 10 things of importance to you	How are they affected by moving?		How are they affected by staying?	
	Short term	Long term	Short term	Long term
1. My family's happiness	will be upset	don't know	not at all	don't know
2. Having a few close friends	will lose friends	probably won't make new ones	not at all	not at all
3. My church affiliation	will be disrupted	will reestablish new affiliation	not at all	not at all
4. My woodworking hobby	a lot of work to pack equipment	maybe bigger space for shop	will continue to complain of not enough space	maybe add on house
5. My parents opinion of how I'm making it	not at all	promotion might increase it	not at all	not at all
6. Having a nice home and car	will be able to buy better home	more money	will continue to feel house is too small	maybe save enough to add on

of a move, but many people (without knowing it) are predicting the first week rather than what happens later on.

John further realized that although his church is important to him, it really is a pretty easily transferred item for him and retains potentially the same meaning. He was initially embarrassed to put woodworking as a prime value. This again is not uncommon: to try to hide a value because we feel it's unimportant in the eyes of those around us. Don't make that error on your chart when you fill it out; put down anything that comes to mind.

In John's case the information he got from his chart was very useful to him and smoothed his decision-making. The decision he came up with is not as important as using the following exercise to provide yourself with additional data for your total thinking about the move.

Once again: relocation is a major decision and you can use all the help and sorting-out mechanisms you can get to take your choice out of the realm of making a decision based purely on "gut feeling." In this exercise, do think of short term effects as one to six months and long term as going beyond that for as long a period as you wish to speculate about.

We can't tell you whether you should give your career or your life style considerations top priority. This is totally up to you. The best way is to combine the two in making the decision. However, here are two examples of families that put life style and personal concerns over career considerations.

One factor in a person's life can be of such importance that it clearly outweighs career and other considerations. John and Mary Sutter's opportunity to transfer was desirable for John's career and they saw no problems in resettling in a new location. Yet they refused transfers because of one concern. It was the deepest concern of their life, the well-being of their retarded son. He was enrolled in an educational program for special children that was unique and he was making excellent progress. Although by refusing a transfer John was

RELOCATION LIFE STYLE VALUE EXERCISE

List 6 to 10 things of importance to you as a style of life

Note what is meaningful to you for each one listed

1. \
2. \
3. \
4. \
5. \
6. \
7. \
8. \
9. \
10.

Evaluate the effects of your relocation decision on each item you listed above.

Item	Effects of moving		Effects of staying	
	Short term	Long term	Short term	Long term
1.				
2.				
3.				
4.				
5.				
6.				
7.				
8.				
9.				
10.				

clearly going to jeopardize his career, this couple was confident that the right thing for them was to stay where they were.

Darryl Clayton was faced with a transfer involving a sizeable promotion and salary increase from a small midwestern town to New York City. He, too, listed the factors that were most important in his life, and it became clear that they were his three sons.

Darryl, after considerable thought and weighing all the other circumstances, decided that, despite the attractions of the new job, what he really wanted to do was to stay right where he was, so he could go to his sons' ball games and be home with them fifteen minutes after work each day. His wife, who had no great desire to cope with the hectic pace of New York life, heartily concurred.

"It may not sound like it" Darryl told us, "but this was the most gutsy decision I ever made in my whole life, and I'm glad I made it—even though many of my colleagues saw it as copping out."

Darryl, like most men, had subscribed to the conventional notion that success on the job should be a man's first concern. It took much soul searching to realize that for him, his relationship with his children was more important than getting to the top in business. This *was* a truly gutsy decision on his part.

Darryl brings up an important point. He says he "doesn't care what his colleagues think."

WHAT'S "GOOD ADVICE" WORTH?

When you are faced with this sort of decision, it's inevitable that you will receive advice and opinions from all sides. Consider these opinions for what they're worth, but do not follow them blindly. The final decision must be yours.

You have now gone through the process of determining how relocation will affect not only your career but your life style goals. Two important by-products flow from this self-examination: (1) it will help you make the best decision, and (2) you will have experienced the fact that you have made a choice.

One of the worst things that can happen in the relocation experience is to think you're being victimized; that even though you don't want to go, you have to. This only leads to lowered work productivity, failure to adjust to the new situation, and difficulty later in getting to feel at home in the new community.

It's important to realize that even those who feel this way *have* made a choice, though they may not be aware of it.

The value of examining your reasons thoroughly is to know why you made your choice. Though there may be drawbacks, you'll realize what they are and what advantages offset them. This knowledge will keep you from feeling helpless or victimized. And who needs that?

MOVE OR YOU'RE THROUGH

Carl Lester was in a quandary. At forty-two, he had just been offered a significant promotion to regional sales manager, but it meant relocation—the last thing he wanted to do at this time.

"I don't want to go for a lot of reasons," he said. "The kids are in school here in Harrisburg, my mother is ill, Mary just started a job that means a lot to her. But I've got to do it."

"Why?" we asked him.

He looked at us with some amazement. "In my company," he said, "if you don't accept promotion when it's offered, you're through. I don't mean they'd fire me or anything like that. But I'd be out of the club. They'd figure I ran out of steam and sort of scratch me off the list of promotable people.

I'd never get another chance—not even in this office. Eventually I'd get shunted aside. I know: I saw it happen to one of the older men here. He refused transfer and the company lost interest in him. Last I heard he'd taken early retirement."

Carl isn't giving his company a chance. He's making an assumption that may be true—but then again, maybe not. The danger is that to assume a negative attitude on the part of the company without checking it out can become a self-fulfilling prophecy. Carl is subscribing to a corporate myth that's rapidly become outmoded.

We tend to anthropomorphize the corporation, visualizing it as an almost human entity with a personality and needs of its own. We think of "the corporation" as the biggest Daddy of them all, the final authority. In the not too distant past, the average corporate employee felt unquestioning, blind obedience to this Daddy was necessary. Many corporate employees feel that the way they "handle the family" during a relocation is a piece of intelligence used by the corporation to help make a final judgment about their suitability for management status.

The sociologist Lionel Tiger likened this phenomenon to tribal rites: "Frequent moves, then, may serve as part of a process of intitiation and testing. . . . it is almost as if all the working notions of the company exist to choose the chief." Whether corporations actually do this is not the point. Some do, some don't. The point is that employees believe it and are consequently threatened by and make their decisions based on this belief.

A corporation is not an entity, certainly not a monolith. It is an aggregation of people, and people change.

As a corporate employee you have choices and you may need to examine and evaluate not only your own career objectives and plan but also your perception of your corporation. How much do you really know about how "it" will behave? How complete and reliable is your data? How much of your information is based on myth, your own needs, or the personality of one supervisor who may soon retire?

POINTS TO REMEMBER

1. Starting out with one company doesn't mean you've signed a life time contract with that company.
2. Ambitions change. The man who wanted to be a captain industry at twenty may want fervently to be captain of his own fishing boat at fifty. Don't let old dreams tie you down.
3. Circumstances change. The couple who could move all over the map when they were childless may have valid reasons for staying put when there's a family to consider. The older couple who resisted moving when the kids were in school may be ready and eager to relocate once the children are grown.

I'VE DECIDED TO STAY—BUT

If you want to stay with the company but aren't eager to move, at least not now, you should also make a sincere effort to explore the alternatives. This does not mean "arguing with the boss." Losers argue. More precisely, arguers who by their belligerent attitude set up an adversary situation with the boss generally lose, no matter how valid their arguments. ("You can't do this to me!" *invites* the response, "Oh, yes we can!")

Winners use *reason* by approaching their managers directly and telling them the reasons they have for not wanting to accept the transfer at this time.

Sample dialogue:

"Jack, the Seattle spot sounds great and I am flattered that I got the call. But at this time it'd really be rough on me and my family to make a move. George is in his junior year and for the first time he's taking hold on finally getting some grades that'll get him into a decent college. Two years ago when Sara went to junior high, Sheri went back to college to finally try to get her B.A. She'd really suffer if she had to give up most of those credits.

"I know the company needs me in Seattle, but do you think I have any alternative? Or do you think we could postpone it for a year or so, at least until George gets off to college?"

How will Henry's manager react to this? We don't know, but in our experience many who take this risk come away with a positive experience and more alternatives than they anticipated.

IT'S THE WRONG PLACE

For Jack, the move's timing was the issue. Sometimes location is the only unacceptable part. For Steve Clay the transfer offer was to North Dakota.

Steve had suffered a minor heart attack at age thirty-eight and was told that exercise was critical for him. For three years he had been jogging regularly five times per week in the morning before work. One can do that in Alabama but, he said, not in North Dakota.

Steve explained why the climate of North Dakota was unacceptable to him and, in fact, a real threat to his health and that he would go to any of the five other corporate sites in warmer climates if the company needed him. Steve's manager had not realized the impact of Steve's condition. He thought Steve's reasons for turning down the transfer were quite valid. After they were reviewed with upper level management, Steve was permitted to stay in his present position with the probability of being offered a promotion to one of the southern sites when a spot opened up.

Corporate acceptance of an employee's wish not to transfer is not as unusual as many people believe. Companies increasingly recognize that an employee who feels coerced into accepting a transfer is ultimately non-productive and costly. Many corporations have asked us to run decision-making workshops for employees who have been asked to transfer. The companies want to insure that employees and their families feel that a move is positive for all involved.

In these workshops, participants assess the effect of the transfer on their career, family life, value system and ability to remain a productive, committed employee. So a growing number of companies realize that the decision to relocate is not easy and that a questioning attitude is valid.

Although most companies provide practical assistance to transferring families, pay moving costs, help them find new homes and the like, the details should be discussed with the business manager or whatever executive is in charge of these arrangements. The employee should clarify *now* the dollars-and-cents aspect of the move so as to avoid unpleasantness or disappointment later. One couple, learning that the company assumed the expenses of house hunting, went for broke. Only later did they learn that there was a strict limitation on what they could spend.

And one more precaution; it's always wise to do a little checking on your own on the state of affairs in the new office. A preliminary get acquainted visit is a good idea. So is a phone call to a friend or acquaintance in that office, whom you can count on to level with you. In most cases, you'll get a "welcome aboard." But there may be bad news: "Look, Charlie, this place is shot to hell. They brought a new division manager in from the East Coast, and he's screwing everything up. Most of the guys are looking for new jobs. I'm looking myself."

POINTS TO REMEMBER

1. Companies are much more open to reason than most employees believe.
2. They're not eager to lose people, if only because much time and money has been invested in longtime employees.

3. They have the answers to practical questions about relocation benefits, but don't necessarily post them on the bulletin board. In one company survey, we found that 30 percent of prospective transferees had questions about benefits that they were afraid to ask management. In another company, we found that an overwhelming number of employees were not utilizing the benefits provided for them.

4. And finally, whether it's about family problems, financial problems, or doubts about the job—tell the truth up front. Don't try to manipulate the company. Management doesn't like to be lied to—no more than you do.

ARE YOU A HIGH RISK OR A LOW RISK MOVER?

Some people take naturally to the mobile life. They seem born to live out of suitcases. Ted and Hillary Woodward are such a couple. In their early thirties, they have already relocated four times, and each move meant a promotion for Ted. Both feel lucky that Ted's job allows (in fact rewards) gypsying. They enjoy discovering new places, sampling new ways of life, and Hillary brags that she can set up housekeeping in a matter of days in whatever house or apartment avails.

"I could do it in a tent," she says, and she probably could.

Yes, there is a Ted, Jr., but he is unaware that there is another way to live since he has spent his entire 3½ years in motion, like an Indian papoose strapped to his mother's back.

We have also come in contact with many teen-agers who have been relocated twelve to twenty times in their fifteen or sixteen years of life. These are youngsters who moved at the same time as their families, sometimes all over the world, sometimes living with parents and sometimes staying in private schools nearby or far away because local schooling was either absent or totally inadequate. Just as with adults, some of these children survive this nomadic life very well; others become seriously impaired.

Ruth Marthwell was fifteen when a private school consulted us to make a routine evaluation of her (among others) for a select foreign exchange program. Ruth had lived in five countries with her parents. Mr. Marthwell is employed by a major oil company, and in fifteen years never lived in the same place for more than two years. His daughter's evaluation showed a very well-adjusted girl with constant curiosity and appetite for new things.

She told us, "Home is wherever I am for more than two weeks. I can't understand why so many of the students here feel sorry for me, why they're unwilling to go wherever the wind takes them. *This* is why they're so uptight! Moving so much has given me an attitude of being able to accept the breaks as they come, good and bad. I intend to work for a company that moves me as much as my father is transferred or I'll marry someone in that position. It gives me the creeps to think of living in the same old house for twenty years."

In our experience, couples like the Woodwards and teen-agers like Ruth are in the minority.

At the other end of the spectrum are families who cannot survive moving. Serious emotional problems, mental break-downs, alcoholism, drug abuse, severe marital discord—all have been precipitated in susceptible people by the stresses of relocation.

THEY COULDN'T HANDLE IT

Jim and Pat Sardi accepted a transfer, their first after five years of marriage and Jim's sixth year with the company. They were excited by the move. They had some apprehension, but felt it would be good experience for them and an excellent career opportunity for Jim. They went through the move pretty well. Their three-year-old daughter seemed to cope uneventfully with the moving chaos, and Jim started his job in good shape.

Now hear what Jim and Pat told us when they consulted us, independently of their corporation, six months after the move. Pat greatly missed her parents, who lived about fifteen minutes from the community they left. She did not feel comfortable with any of her new neighbors and was feeling depressed. Their daughter had become very clinging, difficult to manage and had gotten her sleep schedule mixed up; she was sleeping late and staying up later than Jim and Pat at night.

Jim couldn't understand what was happening, but to stop the "whole thing" he was ready to move back, even if he had to find another job. He described Pat as depressed to the point of not being able to clean house or cook. She was crying constantly.

Jim told us, "It's not worth it, doctor. I'll just give up the damned job. We need to go back home!"

What happened to the Sardis? If we can understand what happened to them, we can arrive at indicators to help predict whether someone is likely to be an extremely high or low risk mover. Keep in mind that Pat and Jim Sardi did want the move.

LOOKING BEHIND THE SCENES

If you had had the following list of facts about Pat and Jim, the story of their relocation outcome would have been a little less surprising:

1. Pat never lived away from home before marrying Jim when she was twenty-three.
2. Her family has lived in their house for sixteen years, moving from only six miles away before that.
3. Her vacations were spent every year (even after marriage) at her parents' beach cottage.
4. Pat and Jim went together for four years while he was in

college and neither dated anyone else during that time.

5. Pat was very close to her three younger sisters and often played the mother or caring-advising role.
6. Jim did go away for a number of summers as a camp counselor, but other than that he also never lived away from home.
7. Both were relatively shy and did not feel comfortable meeting new people.

These are some of the variables in their backgrounds that contributed to their difficulties. On the surface it seems as if Pat had the more difficult adjustment problem, but the profile demonstrates that Jim was unable to take the necessary initiative or provide direction or support to move the two of them to a better adjustment.

HIGH, MIDDLE AND LOW RISK MOVES

Most people are neither extremely high nor low risk movers. Our research has shown that quite a few variables determine whether a person is a high or low risk mover. You can rate yourself to get a picture of your risk profile and to find out what warrants extra thinking or attention.

Read through each of the following variables and rank yourself on the scale on page 51 from 1 (lowest) to 10 (highest) to gauge the degree of importance each variable plays in your life.

Territorial Needs

We all have some degree of need to feel we control some piece of turf, no matter how small, some territory that's ours, safe and (if we want) impenetrable. This need can take on great importance to some people, depending on many personality traits and past experiences. This need is neither "good" nor "bad," but if someone has an extreme need to feel that where he or she lives is inviolate territory (or that certain rooms are almost sacred) that person is probably going to have difficulty moving.

To judge for yourself, ask how adamant you are about having a private place at home; a certain corner of the room; a personal chair; a steady seating place at the dinner table; a workshop that you lock up, etc. If you control such territories, what do you feel about giving any of them up? If you feel your needs are exceptionally strong, rate yourself high on this variable.

Dependency Needs

Just as territorial needs are normal, some dependency needs are part of all of us. Again, they're not positive or negative; they're variables that help you recognize how easy moving may be for you. Dependency means how much do you rely on daily feedback from parents, relatives, or friends to validate your performance? It's a measure of your need for advice and direction from others. Take a look at this for yourself. If you have a high dependency need, judged by how often you ask the advice of certain persons and how difficult it is to make decisions on your own or to initiate something without consultation, this won't help you when you move.

Need for Permanence

Some people are quite comfortable with little sense of permanence in anything around them. Paper plates, paper cups, furniture that can be thrown away instead of repaired, frequent need to change decor, a new car every two years and a philosophy of throw-it-out-if-you-haven't-used-it-in-two years are all indicative of a low need for permanence. You know this variable about yourself, and if you're high in the need for permanence, you're on the high risk side of the scale.

Perceived Choice

How much do you need to feel that you have a choice in whatever you do? Some people refuse to do anything if choice is removed (except for paying taxes). Other people are willing to go along with the notion that others can determine much of what we do. Although we encourage people to be sure they're making the choice to relocate, there often remains a sense of, "Yes, we made the choice, but when it comes down to it the alternatives seemed so risky that we really had no choice." If you're the kind of person who just cannot tolerate the feeling of choice being taken away, you may have difficulty moving. Think of this need in some other aspects of your life. If you really don't care what you eat when you're asked what you want; if you're willing to let your spouse or friend tell you what clothes look good on you; if you often say "I don't care" when you're given a choice, the chances are you don't rate high on the scale of always needing to perceive yourself as having choices. So you also rank low as a relocation risk in this respect.

Separation Anxiety

Being away from the familiar, from people you trust, often causes feelings of loss of predictability and security. People vary widely in their tolerance for this, and we have found that those who experience relatively high separation anxiety are often the same people who have great difficulty with relocation. Some of the signs of separation anxiety are unwillingness to place yourself in a position of being away from family; reluctance to try new things when it means giving up old ones; discomfort when alone. You can probably think of other such discomforts in your own experience.

Need for Relatedness

The need for relatedness is the experience of feeling tied into things, having anchors for yourself. This need varies greatly in people. Some need to feel that they know where and what everything around them is. They have a relationship with the people as well as the things in their environment. Relatedness is also a need to feel that what you believe (your attitudes and values) is validated and for the most part supported by your surroundings. This is one of the most disrupted needs when a significant cultural change accompanies a relocation. Exceptionally high need for relatedness points to a high risk mover, especially if you're off to a very different cultural or social environment.

Marital Stress

If you're married, your relationship with your spouse is a critical variable as an indicator of relocation risk. Relocation is rarely responsible for a marriage disintegration. But a deteriorating marriage can be pushed over the line by the added stress of relocating. Just as having a baby is never a solution to a shaky marriage, neither is relocation. Marriages that are under great stress prior to a transfer usually bring on difficult relocations. People in that situation should rate themselves as high risk movers in this variable.

Support Systems

Some folks are loners, others need to be members of groups and feel they belong to clusters that help them identify themselves. Organizations, churches, clubs and other social groups make up our formal support systems. We can also gather less formal support systems through close friendships. Most people need this base to some extent, but if you feel you're extremely needy of strong, unvarying support systems, this would tend to make you a high risk mover in this variable. Moderate need in this section can be very effective for successful relocation.

Extended Family Need

This is a pretty easy variable to judge yourself on. How close do you feel you need to be, geographically, to parents, siblings and other relatives? Again, there is no "right" or "wrong." If you're moving away from family and feel you have a high need for closeness with them, you can imagine that relocation will be difficult. If you have a high need and relocation means moving closer to family this may make it easier.

HIGH-LOW RELOCATION RISK SCALE

Personality Variables	High Need									Low Need
	10	9	8	7	6	5	4	3	2	1
Territorial Needs										
Dependency Needs										
Permanence										
Perceived choice										
Separation Anxiety										
Need for Relatedness										
Marital Stress										
Support Systems										
Extended Family Need										

Note: all the foregoing personality variables are related here to relocation adjustment. *Do not* confuse them with emotional adjustment or mental health. These are not positive or negative qualities. They only indicate needs that play a role in how easy it is to move.

Please use discretion in interpreting the profile you come up with for yourself. If you rate high in a particular need but by moving you find that you gain more ways of gratifying the need, simply reverse its value. For example, if you rated yourself 9 on need for closeness to family and moving in fact brings you closer, it is not a high risk variable for you for that particular move.

If three or more variables are scored 8, 9 or 10, you should seriously consider that you may have a difficult time relocating. Putting yourself into a high risk category requires at least three variables scored 8, 9 or 10. Do not consider any of this decisive! It should serve as a warning signal, problems to work on.

Russ Harrington, a forty-two-year-old vice-president of operations for a moderate size corporation, was asked to transfer to the West Coast from the Atlanta office in a move involving several departments. Russ had never moved before and was very concerned. He felt he might be a high risk mover. His wife, Jane, was also concerned. Among the many other assessments they used in our workshop, they filled out the following High-Low Relocation Risk Scale.

Jane scored 9 on only one variable, and for the most part both do not score as high risk movers, despite their anticipation of being in that category. Jane needed to feel that she was in control of whether they decided to go and that it truly was their choice. Russ and Jane worked on this, and once they were convinced they were making the choice for themselves and it was not the company dictating, she felt quite relieved.

The High-Low Relocation Risk Scale gave them a profile of what they needed to discuss and focus on in their adjust-

RUSS'S HIGH-LOW RELOCATION RISK SCALE

Personality Variables	High Need									Low Need
	10	9	8	7	6	5	4	3	2	1
Territorial Needs								x		
Dependency Needs						x				
Permanence								x		
Perceived choice			x							
Separation Anxiety								x		
Need for Relatedness		x								
Marital Stress										x
Support Systems							x			
Extended Family Need						x				

JANE'S HIGH-LOW RELOCATION RISK SCALE

Personality Variables	High Need									Low Need
	10	9	8	7	6	5	4	3	2	1
Territorial Needs						x				
Dependency Needs							x			
Permanence			x							
Perceived Choice		x								
Separation Anxiety						x				
Need for Relatedness							x			
Marital Stress										x
Support Systems							x			
Extended Family Need								x		

ment to the new community. Most of all it helped them to free themselves from a preconceived notion of being high risk movers.

Presumably, you have now rated yourself on nine personality variables and come up with a profile of risk for yourself in relocating. A number of other factors contribute to your relative mobility, and the following questionnaire combines many aspects of your experience to give you still another assessment of your own degree of risk. Just as you used the High-Low Relocation Risk Scale, this Relocation Risk Questionnaire will give you an opportunity to think about the issues and see how you compare with others.

ARE YOU A HIGH RISK MOVER?

Rate on a scale of 1 to 10 how accurately these statements apply to you. A score of 10 means that a statement totally, unequivocally applies to you; a score of 1 means that it doesn't apply at all.

1. I'm very close to my parents.
2. Most of my close friends are people I've known since school.
3. I don't like to go to parties unless I know most of the people there.
4. I'm just no good at small talk; I can't make conversation unless it's about something important.
5. I don't like changes in routine. I plan my time very carefully, and it upsets me when I have to change those plans.
6. I like meeting new people, but I'm sometimes afraid they won't like me.
7. I'm pretty cautious about money, better a safe savings account than fooling around in the stock market.
8. I don't see what people see in gambling games. I'd be afraid I'd lose.

9. I'm uncomfortable with people who are better educated or richer than I am.
10. I'm uncomfortable with people who are less well educated, or have less money than I do.
11. I'm uncomfortable with people from a different ethnic background.
12. I worry a lot about what other people think.
13. My children are very important to me. Their schooling comes first in our family.
14. My home is very important to me. I have put a lot of effort into improving it and decorating it.
15. Possessions are very important to me. I guess I'm a pack rat—I save things.
16. I can't bear to throw out old appliances. If a toaster doesn't work, I send it back to the company.
17. I think it's stupid to keep buying new clothes. I invest in what looks good on me, then keep wearing it, whatever the new fashion is.
18. It's a waste of money to eat in restaurants, except for very special occasions.
19. I always vote the straight party line.
20. I can't imagine living anywhere outside the United States.
21. I like watching television, but I'd be terrified if I had to appear on it.
22. I prefer not to travel to different places on vacation and would rather return to the same spot each year.
23. I have not moved successfully before.

WHAT YOUR SCORE MEANS

Add up your score. If it's between 150 and 230, you're probably a high risk mover. This doesn't mean you're in any way a deficient person. Scoring high on thrift, preparedness and economy definitely puts you in the virtuous category. It just means that moving is harder on you than on other people.

If you scored between 23 and the low 100s, you're definitely a low risk mover. The really low score does not imply anything good or bad either, it's just a clue that you probably will not be taking too much of a risk by relocating.

"GUESS WHAT, HONEY, WE'RE MOVING!"

Typically, the husband is the first to know, although (the office and corporate wives' grapevine being what it is) his wife almost surely suspects well ahead of time that Fred may be offered sales manager in East Allensburg.

The tension can start building long before the offer is made. She doesn't know whether to be sad or glad. It's a big step up in the company for Fred. On the other hand, she's just learned to like it in New Rochelle. She dreads the thought of pulling up stakes and starting all over again in a new, strange city. She doesn't want to hold Fred back (that's being a *bad wife*), and yet, and yet . . . her friends are here, her neighbors, her part-time job, the proximity of New York City with its bazaar of cultural delights—East Allensburg indeed!—not to mention the herb garden she had started from seedlings.

And so she holds her peace. The gods will decide. She doesn't mention the possible move to Fred. Why look for trouble? Nor does he mention it to her (although all her friends are doing so) for the same reason. He remembers how unhappy she was over the previous move.

When the decision is made and the boss tells Fred he's been tapped for the East Allensburg job, his first reaction is usually pride and delight at being selected. Any personal qualms about relocating are momentarily obscured by the handsome raise and the validation that he is moving up the corporate ladder. What he does have qualms about is Nancy. He feels simultaneously guilty about asking her to move once again, genuinely concerned about her reaction, and a little nervous about how to break the news.

This dilemma is all too often solved by stopping off on the way home for a few drinks with office buddies to celebrate his promotion and get up the courage to announce to Nancy (as he arrives an hour late for dinner), "Guess what, honey, we're moving!"

Dead silence from Nancy.

"East Allensburg, I presume," she then says, wishing to spoil the surprise.

"How did you know?" says Fred.

Nancy sighs. "*Everybody* has known for months. Well, congratulations, I guess. When do we start packing?"

Fred says, "Wait a minute, honey! It's not all that bad. I'm sales manager, I get a $5,000 raise, and you're just going to *love* it in East Allensburg!"

"I'm just going to *hate* it in East Allensburg! But what do I count for in this marriage. . . ."

Experienced movers can fill in the rest of this dismal dialogue for themselves. Unfortunately, this kind of situation is all too familiar.

This initial discussion of the relocation is one of the most significant indicators of how each family member will feel throughout the transfer. Like Fred, the feelings of guilt, concern and uncertainty are among the least acknowledged by the corporations, colleagues and friends. Our experiences have taught us that the typical man goes through very deep feelings about the potential impact of a relocation on his wife and family, yet he has little acceptable format or male peer permission for expressing these feelings.

Caught between total denial of the guilt or the "disgrace" of risking that he'll appear "soft" in front of his male corporate friends, a thumping internal turmoil often develops. Unfortunately, knowing no other way, the man comes home and tries to sell the transfer just as Fred did to Nancy, which is the surest way to make a partner feel left out of a family decision.

THE RASHOMON SYNDROME

Fred and Nancy have a serious case of what we call the *Rashomon syndrome.* If you saw the Japanese motion picture *Rashomon,* you'll recall that it presented two versions of a marital conflict, one from the wife's point of view, one from the husband's. The facts of the situation were identical; the interpretations drawn from these facts varied considerably.

The film is more than an evening's entertainment. It gets to the root cause of practically all relationship problems— the inability to see things from the other person's point of view. The other person can be a parent or a child, a boss or employee, a relative, co-worker, friend, or a spouse.

When you're under stress keep in mind that marital communications change, style of talking changes, and finding the same wavelength becomes more difficult .The danger is that stressed communications that only have to do with relocation problems can be misinterpreted as general marital stress.

The husband and wife afflicted with Rashomonitis probably have the most difficult problem, because it is compounded by gender differences, power differentials and the rapidly changing roles of women and men in society.

There's a further possible complication, and it's an ironic one. Partners who care deeply for each other will often try to *anticipate* each other's desires on the basis of well-meaning misconceptions.

A husband may, for example, turn down a transfer because he's sure his wife doesn't *really* want to go, even though she says she does. Or she may pretend she doesn't want to move because she thinks he doesn't. No matter how benign the motivation, the upshot is a muddle.

The specific cure for Rashomonitis is a strong dose of mutual understanding. And the first step in the treatment is to find out the other person's point of view.

SEEING HER SIDE OF IT

The corporate wife may be many women. She may be the bride of the fifties, who married believing that her only role in life was full-time housekeeper, mother and backstop to her husband. She may be the bride of the sixties, who put her own career aspirations on "hold" until the children were grown. Or she may be a bride of the seventies, who signed a marriage contract full of stipulations about who is supposed to do what household chores. But these are textbook models. Most often, whether she's twenty-two or fifty-two, she is a combination of all three, influenced in varying degrees by tradition, inner needs and her growing awareness of women's rights.

What she definitely is is a person in her own right. And what she wants is equal partnership with her husband in marriage, child raising and in his (their) career(s).

We have found that the concerns of corporate wives about relocation stem from eight more or less obvious sources:

1. the practical inconvenience of moving
2. separation from friends, family and familiar community
3. feeling left out of decision-making
4. fear of hurting children

5. fear of what pressures a move or new job may put on an already over pressured husband
6. the effect the move will have on her own personal development (including career and educational plans)
7. fear of demands that a move up the corporate ladder may place on her
8. jealousy

It's difficult for a wife to deal with a husband who is a "workaholic." Telling him that he's working too hard (and should take it easy) only complicates their life. He probably knows this already. If she reiterates the point, she merely compounds his anxiety.

The fear of demands that a move up the corporate ladder may make on a wife is difficult for her to express. Typically, this woman feels socially inadequate. She fears that she'll be unable to meet on an equal level with families higher up in the corporate hierarchy and therefore will become an embarrassment to her husband.

And jealous of what? not of other women (corporate men almost invariably put business first) or the husband's success. No, she's jealous of the company itself. Nancy, our prototypical wife, knows that she is first in Fred's affections, that his job is her career too. But she worries, quite realistically, that her chief competitor for his loyalty is the corporation. Her remark, "What do I count for in this marriage?" is a dead giveaway.

Lady Bird Johnson, a very wise woman, once observed, accurately if cynically, that all politicians should be born orphans and remain celibate. Mrs. Johnson knew what she was talking about. The man who is wedded to his job encounters a certain number of predictable difficulties; he is also wedded to a woman about whom he cares a great deal. But there are no difficulties that can't be resolved by mutual understanding, trust, and open communication.

THE WIFE HE MARRIED WHEN YOUNG

The executive on the way up usually sees his wife as much the same girl he married fifteen years ago. As a bride, she dedicated her life to him. As a young wife, she took her identity from her husband's job (even if she did make him help with the housework).

While women change and grow, even as do men, the man who has worked his way up from an entry level job to middle management (or better) often does not realize that his bride of fifteen years ago has also developed from a girl into a mature woman. The prospect of a relocation may force them both to confront her changing need system.

Sarah Dixon married Bill Evans when she was eighteen, just out of high school and determined not to spend her life in Dubuque, Iowa (as her two older sisters were destined to), one block away from her very dominant mother. Bill, who was twenty-six and a fast-tracked marketing manager with a large corporation, was a natural for Sarah. In the early years of their marriage Sarah completely identified with Bill's fast corporate climb; their success enabled Sarah to justify being the first Dixon to leave Dubuque, incurring family disapproval.

She accepted the first three transfers, which all came within six years, eagerly and gracefully. Six years later, when the company asked the Evanses to move from Hartford, Connecticut to Boston (representing another notch in Bill's corporate belt), Sarah found herself unenthusiastic, uncertain and not very eager to accept the transfer. Sarah was unable to articulate the reasons for her change in attitude, and when the couple came to our workshop Bill expressed annoyance, impatience and concern: "We need to make a decision and Sarah can't tell me what's changed her attitude."

With the help of some exercises the Evanses were able to understand what had happened. In the twelve years since they were married Sarah was successfully mothering two children and managed to get her B.A., despite three moves. In Hartford, she was being considered for promotion with a large insurance company. On top of this, over time, Sarah's parents had become more accepting of her life style. Sarah's growing self-identity had made contacts with her parents less threatening, and that relationship was getting close. In short, Sarah no longer needed Bill's success to be comfortable with herself.

Bill and Sarah did decide to accept the move; they did so with confidence in their decision and a solid mutual understanding of Sarah's changed need system. This enabled them to plan how Sarah's and Bill's needs could both be met in the future.

She may not have had a career comparable to his. But she has managed a home, cared for children, participated in community activities, and often did some paid work. In the process, she developed a strong sense of her *own* identity. Her marriage vows said, "For better, for worse, for richer, for poorer." They did not include "And for the greater glory of Allied Chemical."

Her mature identity is questioned or negated when she is told, as if she were a child, that it's time to get packing and get moving—the company says so.

The Freds (from our example at the beginning of this chapter) who don't realize this are often faced by rebellious Nancys, who either move sulkily or with unexpressed anger, or refuse to move at all leading to a degeneration or disintegration of the marriage.

GO ON, TELL HER!

The employee who senses that a move may be impending should take his nearest and dearest into his confidence immediately. Sample dialogue:

FRED: It's a lot too soon to even talk about it, but rumor has it that I'm being put up for the East Allensburg job.

NANCY: I know.

FRED: You know? How do *you* know?

NANCY: Ethel Garroway told me.

FRED: Ethel *Garroway*! What does she know about it?

NANCY: She *thinks* she knows everything about it.

FRED: [irritably] Gossip, gossip, gossip.

NANCY: Okay, gossip, gossip! But it's true, isn't it?

FRED: I guess so. But don't get your hopes up. There are several contenders for this job.

NANCY: I'm not getting my hopes up. I'm certainly not crazy about pulling up stakes and moving. It's more your hopes. Do you really want the job?

FRED: I think so. But I'm not sure, not till I know more about it. Besides, it'd be putting us through one more move. Maybe we've had enough already. And I'm certainly not going to take it unless you think it's a good idea.

NANCY: Fred, you know that if you get the job and it's the right one, I'm with you all the way. I learned to like New Rochelle and I can learn to like East Allensburg. We're partners, remember?

FRED: Partners, right. Nancy, you're the greatest.

Fred feels relieved; Nancy has been included. The agony of waiting is easier when there are two to share it. Besides, he feels free of the extra worry that Nancy will balk at moving. Nancy's "left out" feeling has been dissipated. The waiting time gives her time to get her head together. If the move turns out to be the right move, she's mentally preparing herself to adjust to it. If Fred's hopes are dashed and he doesn't get the job—she stands ready to bind up his wounds. What's a good wife for?

WHEN THE JOB IS FINALLY YOURS

Let's skip forward to the day the boss tells Fred that the job is his, if he wants it.

At this point, some Freds forget all about the partnership, as well as the normal precautions any transferee should take before committing himself to a move.

Sample scenario: Fred has gotten the good news, accepts the job on the spot and phones Nancy to get a sitter and meet him downtown for the victory dinner.

When Nancy arrives at the restaurant, Fred is beaming over his martini.

"We made it, honey!" he says, "I got the job. I'm the fair-haired boy! Waiter, bring me another one of these and one for the lady."

"Fred, that's wonderful!" Nancy says, "I'm so proud of you."

"You're happy about it, aren't you?" Fred says. "I mean, I wouldn't have taken the job if I thought you wouldn't be happy about it."

"I am deliriously happy about it," Nancy says. "The hell with New Rochelle. Here we come, East Allensburg." They raise their glasses in a toast.

"You know," says Fred, "You should have been at the office today when the news broke. I mean, you should have seen the look on Ed Garroway's face."

Nancy, who can hardly wait to see the look on Ethel Garroway's face, claps her hands in glee.

She Gets Down to Business

Two martinis later and halfway through her filet mignon, Nancy gets down to business.

NANCY: So let's have the details. Is it really a $5,000 raise?

FRED: Well, you know, I didn't stop to quibble about

money. But it's some kind of raise—I mean, it's got to be. I mean, sales manager . . .

NANCY: Oh, sure, it's got to be more money. But are you really going to be running your own show—I mean, no strings sales manager?

FRED: Well, I *suppose* so. Ed Rasmussen was, the guy who had the job before me.

NANCY: Ed Rasmussen got fired.

FRED: Will you quite being a wet blanket? Ed Rasmussen was stupid. Everybody in the company knows *that*.

NANCY: Okay, Okay. You're the expert on office politics. Pardon me for asking.

FRED: That's all right, honey. You have a right to know. You have a stake in this too.

Nancy, who is about ready at this point to sell out her claim, retreats.

"Well," she says, "When does the move take place? We have to find a house, you know. How much time have we got? Who's going to move us? What does the company pay for and what are we going to do with the New Rochelle house?"

"No problem," says Fred. "No problem at all. I have to go out to Kansas at the end of the week, so you can just get started on the detail stuff. I mean, the company pays for the move, so just call up somebody—Al Olsen, I think. Or maybe it's Al Johnson. Just call Al and he'll tell you what to do. There's some real estate company that's supposed to show us houses. Ask Al who they are. Get busy packing and *please*, don't forget to arrange the special packing for my antique tools the way you did last time."

What Did Fred Do Wrong?

Just about everything. And not only for peace in his partnership with Nancy, but also for his own career interests.

He accepted the transfer without learning what the exact setup of the job was or even the exact salary. Amazing! Yet it happens all the time. Next, why did Ed Rasmussen really get fired? That's important to know.

Fred also didn't have a clue about the practical details of relocation, not the exact company policy on moving nor even the correct name of the man in charge of such matters. That, he left up to good old Nancy, along with assigning her personal responsibility for the safety of his antique tool collection.

To nonmovers, this may all sound like a family life TV sit-com that's about to be cancelled.

To experienced movers, it's all too true to life. We've heard worse than this from irate Nancys, who are not only convinced that their husbands are being led astray by a fickle mistress, the company, but that they're being forced into servitude as lady's maid.

AND NOW: THE BETTER WAY

There is, of course, a better way. After getting the job offer, Fred should have first talked it all over with his boss, ascertaining the exact salary and the exact job responsibilities. Bosses are willing to explain these things, if asked. (They often don't think it's necessary; they assume the employee knows.)

Again, why did Ed Rasmussen get fired? is a perfectly legitimate question. This may seem improper to some Freds, but it will command at least the respect of the executive of whom it is asked. (Much of this reasoning was explained in chapter 3—but it never hurts to reinforce important points.)

Fred should inquire at that point about company moving benefits, or at least get the name of the person with the information.

He should close the interview on a positive note. "Henry,

it sounds pretty good to me. But, of course, I'll need some time to think on it and to talk it over with Nancy."

Henry: "Oh, naturally, naturally. [If Fred had accepted on the spot, Henry might well have written him off as a damn fool.] Take all the time you want. Well, not *all* the time. We do have to know within the week. And give my love to Nancy."

Fred does just that when he arrives home for dinner and tells her that the offer has finally come through.

NANCY: Is it what you thought?

FRED: Well, mostly. It's a $3,000 raise, not $5,000. And it's sales manager, but not with the free hand Ed Rasmussen had or tried to take. Rasmussen is a great guy, but he likes to run the show his own way. It was a sort of personality clash thing between him and the district manager, Doug Feiffer.

NANCY: Oh, I remember him from Chicago. He's nice.

FRED: Well, I always got along with him. So what do you say, Nancy?

NANCY: Well, I say let's go! It's not as much money as we thought, but then it's cheaper to live out there.

FRED: But what about your garden club?

NANCY: Sure, I'll miss it. Hey, how old is Doug Feiffer? I mean, he should be retiring soon, shouldn't he?

FRED: *Nancy*! I'm surprised at you!

NANCY: Well, you're always saying, "be practical." So I'm being practical. If Doug retires in the next few years, you get his job, right?

FRED: Well, there's a lot more to it than that. Meanwhile, I better not invite Doug to dinner—Ms. Borgia here might just poison him.

NANCY: The one without the parsley is the one without the poison.

FRED: [Opening his briefcase and taking out a wad of

papers] Come on, Nancy, let's get practical about getting the show on the road. Now, you can see the company will assume the costs of moving *and* underwrite the sale of the old house, so . . .

And so, Nancy and Fred spend an idyllic evening by the fire, reading the fine print, making positive plans for their move and enjoying the whole thing immensely.

SEEING HIS SIDE OF IT

How many times have your heard: "The man has it easy in a relocation! He's got a ready-made comfort zone: his job and office friends. The wife has to worry about the whole family." Our workshops dramatically show that this popular view of relocation is just not the way it works.

The man who is wedded to his job encounters a certain number of predictable conflicts when he is also wedded to a woman about whom he cares a great deal.

The man who is about to be moved has three primary concerns:

1. Anxiety about the job itself. Will he perform well? Has he made the right choice?
2. Unhappiness about leaving his friends, his social group, a community of which he has become a part.
3. Concern about the impact of the move on his family.

We are continually impressed with the amount of anxiety most men experience about changing jobs. Unfortunately, peer pressure, and role expectations make it difficult to express the depth of feeling men have about this issue, so the feelings are often expressed indirectly.

John Plessey worked with a small corporate division in Florida that was being relocated and merged with corporate headquarters in Boston because innovative marketing efforts had netted startlingly high profits for the division.

John's company was providing very liberal relocation benefits, yet John started our workshop by complaining how some uncovered items proved to him that the company was mishandling the entire relocation.

"They're paying $30,000 to buy my house, cover my mortgage differential, and find me a new house, but they won't pay $300 to ship my second car," ranted John. "The three days of work I'll have to take off to drive the damn car are worth three times that much. It doesn't make sense!"

John's next statement was the tip-off to what he really was upset about. "In Florida, when something like this came up, I walked down the hall and talked to Joe Dixon, our personnel manager. He straightened it out in two minutes. Now I don't even know who to talk to." This led John to express his feelings and fears about the merger, his real concern.

John was concerned about his new boss's attitudes; policies at the corporate level; and, mostly, the loss of the small-company feeling and pride of accomplishment that he enjoyed in Florida.

John's depth of feeling about changing jobs is typical; a smart and caring wife will try to understand this and how it is affecting her husband's behavior.

In the case of Fred and Nancy Smith, it was the husband riding roughshod over his wife's legitimate needs. Sometimes, as many divorced men will testify, it's the wife who won't play fair.

JEANNIE HAS HER FANTASIES

Let's forget Fred and Nancy for a while, and consider Al and Jeannie Green. Like Nancy, Jeannie has heard via the grapevine that her husband is in line for a move. Unlike Nancy, she has not kept quiet about it. She has taken off on her own fantasies long before the move became a reality. Sample before-the-fact dialogue:

JEANNIE: *Well*—I hear you're in for a big promotion.

AL: Where did you hear that Jeannie?

JEANNIE: Didi Fassbinder told me all about it. They need new sales managers in Houston and in Miami and San Francisco. Didi says you're the obvious choice for one of the jobs, and that it's going to mean a big raise.

AL: Didi Fassbinder doesn't work for the company, how does she know?

JEANNIE: Well, she should—her husband's in personnel, isn't he?

AL: Look Jeannie, we can't live our lives on Didi's rumor mill so just forget it! Did you take the dog to the vet today?

JEANNIE: No, I didn't get a chance.

AL: Say, you don't suppose Didi really knows?

JEANNIE: She was right about Chuck Campbell and Dick Carson.

AL: Wouldn't that be something; how would you feel about it?

JEANNIE: I'd *love* it. I mean, I know you like New Rochelle, but I've had somewhat of a rough time here. We've been living here for three years and I haven't been able to make any friends. The only one I'm a little close to is Didi Fassbinder. I really feel out of place. Everyone in this neighborhood is high up in their company or a professional. Sometimes it gets to me, and I don't understand why it doesn't get to you.

AL: Look honey, I'm trying to move up. I'm doing the best I can.

JEANNIE: Al, I'm sorry, I didn't mean it that way.

AL: Okay, Okay, well, at least we both agree we want to move.

NOW: THE REALITY

Let's look forward to the day when the transfer becomes a reality. Al comes home without stopping for any celebration drinks along the way to tell the good news to Jeannie.

AL: Guess what, honey, we're moving!

JEANNIE: You got the job! You got the *job*! Come on, sit down and tell me all about it. Which is it, California or Texas?

AL: Something even better. It's the West Platsville plant, in the Chicago area.

JEANNIE: *Chicago*? That doesn't sound so great.

AL: Well, let me explain. The middle west is our strongest sales area, and the Chicago sales manager is first in line for regional sales manager.

JEANNIE: So what about the money?

AL: [expansively] Well, I get a $5,000 raise to start and after that, who knows!

JEANNIE: When they moved Burt McIlhenny to the New York office, he got a $10,000 raise.

AL: Sweetie, Burt McIhhenny is eighteen years older than I am and he was being moved up to vice-president.

JEANNIE: They have some vice-presidents who're younger than you, like Allen Carmody.

AL: [patiently] Allen Carmody is the chairman of the board's nephew. Please, Jeannie, try to understand.

JEANNIE: I am trying. Believe me, Al, I am trying. But don't forget, I don't have as much education as you do.

AL: Now what is that supposed to mean?

JEANNIE: All I have is a B.A. You have a masters in business administration. I gave up graduate school for you. If I had stayed with it, like Myrna Eberhard did, I could be making $60,000 a year as a clinical psychologist. I went to school with Lily Benedict. She didn't get married and now she has published a novel. Maybe I shouldn't have gotten married in the first place.

AL: Maybe you shouldn't.

IS THE COMPANY THE VILLAIN?

While this conversation may sound contrived, it's representative of what happens to many couples. On the surface, Jeannie seems to be nagging Al and is dissatisfied with him and her marriage. Marital conflicts often arise around a relocation, and we advise couples to evaluate how much of the conflict represents relocation and job related concerns. Jeannie and Al attended one of our workshops and discovered what was really behind that seemingly negative interaction.

Jeannie was finally able to express that she felt that Al was being mistreated by his company and that the move to Chicago, rather than L.A. or Dallas, represented the company's low regard for Al. Jeannie's caring for Al prevented her from expressing these feelings because she felt it would hurt him too much. Jeannie's assumption that a job offer in Chicago represented low regard for Al was erroneous and based on her perception that the image of an area rather than the job reflected the company's attitude.

This issue was handled differently by Madeline Roberts who told us, "Of course I love my husband. And I'm always willing to move with him—providing of course it's a town we're going to enjoy living in. But just because I do love him, I can't stand seeing him pushed around by the company, sent to awful out-of-the-way places, or not getting the recognition other men get. And I feel it's my duty to say so."

To attempt to analyze briefly what made Jeannie and

Madeline react as they did is not necessary or possible. The point is that problems between husband and wife are not always one-sided with the husband the bad guy. Jeannie and Madeline have their own perceptions of life, which may be based on unrealistic aspirations or the frustration that frequent relocations often create in women.

Jeannie, like many women, had to sacrifice education, career and personal goals for the sake of her husband's career. An unhappy relocation to an undesirable area or a slower than hoped for career path can sometimes suddenly bring a woman's cumulative frustrations to the fore all at once. It is easy at this point to blame her husband, feel victimized and become hostile, critical and undermining.

Madeline realized that her focus on her husband's career really reflected the frustration she felt because five relocations had delayed the completion of her M.S.W. While her concern for her husband and the treatment he was receiving by his company was genuine, her own frustrations were leading her to express hostility in an unproductive way.

"BUT WE CAN'T TAKE JOHNNY OUT OF SCHOOL"

What happens to Johnny and school? This is perhaps the most commonly asked question by parents facing a move. The cry that Johnny "can't be taken out of school" is easy to understand and reflects parents' concern about a child's education. The apprehension about school is real, but the question also acts, as a safe way of expressing other not so conscious or easily talked about concerns about moving the child.

Comments about changing schools or teachers are also commonly heard from children when they're told of a move. Again, some of the concerns expressed are school-related, but they also serve as camouflage for the child, just as they do for his parents. Complaints about teacher changes are the safest and most approved way, in the child's eyes, to express feelings about the move.

Some people would like us to believe that relocations have no effect on children and should be treated as inconsequential to their development. This is a real misunderstanding of effect and of the life of a child. It's difficult to see a child as a lesser entity than an adult and as not influenced—postively or negatively—by the same events. Oh, a child's expressions are different and some aspects of the move that a child responds to may be different. But if children are alive, react they must.

Some parents' denials of potential effects on children stem from guilt. We have done everything possible in our society to help parents feel guilty about every interaction they have with their children and it's understandable that many have to deny any effects just to prevent guilt from becoming overwhelming. The most important point we can make for you as a parent is that we can be sure the child will have reactions (maybe not right away) to a move, but the effects can be made positive and the events of the relocation can be used constructively.

Tom and Lilly Wilson were kind enough to respond to our questionnaire and to correspond with us about their experiences. They presented their moves in a positive way and initially responded to our questionnaire that they wanted to contribute "the good side of moving" to our research.

Mrs. Wilson wrote in a recent letter, "It must be very refreshing for you two to know *one* family that isn't the least bit neurotic about moving. Sure, we'll miss Pittsburgh, but you better believe we'll have plenty of house guests in Florida. And it's really terrific for the kids. They've got really good schools, there's swimming all year round and *no air pollution.*"

We sent another set of questions and asked them to comment on whether Liza and Tommy are happy about their move.

WHY IS TOMMY WETTING HIS BED?

Mrs. Wilson wrote back with a long letter expressing surprise at our question. Essentially, she guessed that they were, "I mean, what is there for kids in Pittsburgh? Oh, Liza has been moping around about her girlfriends and her dance class or whatever, but then she's seven. It's a difficult age, but she'll get over it. Tommy, on the other hand, hasn't said a word. Five year olds are such wonderful little creatures. They adjust to anything.

"By the way," she said, "not to change the subject, but maybe you can give us some advice. Tommy, for no apparent reason, has started to wet his bed. Do you know a good child psychologist in Florida?"

SILENCE ISN'T CONSENT

We did, and we gave Lilly her name. We haven't heard again from the Wilsons, but we're confident that this very skilled and sympathetic woman counselor will be able to help with a problem that's not Tommy's, but his parents'.

Children, merely because they *are* children, are much more vulnerable to the traumas of relocation than adults. Even preschoolers have formed attachments to the environment they're familiar with. Being taken out of it is inevitably a fearsome thing, even if they can't articulate their fears. *Especially* if they can't express their fears, as in the case of bed-wetting Tommy, to whom Pittsburgh was home, air pollution and all.

Furthermore, children stand in double jeopardy. Because too many parents (Tom and Lilly are a good example) tend to dismiss the youngsters' half-voiced miseries by assuming that they'll get over them, without expressing and understanding the problems.

Archie and Claudia Nelson were very excited about a transfer from Westchester County, New York to a rural community in upstate New York about 400 miles away. They were happy to have the chance to get "out of the rat race." They stood to make a significant amount of money on their home and could purchase in the new area for much less.

Their three children, aged nine, thirteen, and fourteen,

listened to the news as Archie presented all the great things about the new home. The two younger ones were excited and asked questions, but fourteen-year-old Todd said nothing. For the next three weeks he moped around, ate little and really seemed depressed.

Archie, an ardent magazine reader in his daily train commute to New York City, was well aware of the need to have a father and son talk. So he did. Todd told him he did not want to move because he had a girlfriend.

"Oh, I know how you feel, but you're too young for that and there are lots of girls in Oswego," his Dad said. "You'll get over it very quickly, I'm sure. Just think of the fun fishing in all those streams and lakes."

Archie, a genuinely interested father, walked away feeling he had done a good thing with his son. Indeed, Archie did more than many. He recognized a problem, went to Todd, asked questions, but he committed an error that's easy for parents to make. Surely Todd had a case of puppy love. Archie figured Todd could look at it that way. For Todd, his love for his girlfriend is a most serious matter, and parents in this situation have to acknowledge that in some way.

HERE'S A BETTER WAY

Archie might have avoided the negative reactions that Todd showed for six months after the move. Archie might have said, "Todd, I had no idea you felt strongly about a girl. I know this is going to be tough, but I'll stick with you man to man to help you with it. If it's something you do not want Mom or your sisters to know about, don't worry. I'll keep this to myself and we'll keep working at it until we come up with some answers."

More discussion must take place, but the direction that will really help Todd is set: his feelings are acknowledged as deep and important. The father recognizes that separation will be difficult, but he'll do all he can to help Todd figure out ways to keep the relationship alive. The fact that 99 percent of puppy love situations die in two to three months is not mentioned at all.

Any feeling of concern that children express should be treated seriously and never dismissed as foolish or immature. Will they get over it? Sometimes they do. Sometimes they don't.

There are horror stories of frequently uprooted children who developed problems much worse than bed-wetting: drug addiction, teen-age promiscuity, petty crime, even major crime. The prison population of America is largely made up of people with unhappy childhoods.

Translation: they had no opportunity to grow roots, too little chance to establish an identity.

For that reason, some social analysts have condemned moving, across the board. With due respect the basic problem isn't relocation; it's *badly* handled relocation.

And that's where parents come into it. Moving *per se* isn't the problem. Being uprooted is. Much of the prison population consists of individuals who were uprooted without leaving their own hometowns; by parental indifference, neglect or abandonment.

HOW TO TRANSPLANT A CHILD

Compare your child to a plant. If you pull up a small tree by its roots and throw it in a moving van, it's going to die. But if you ball it, pack it and wrap it in burlap, you can transplant it to a new location where it may do even better!

First of all, open up communications about the move immediately. The best and easiest way is to call a family conference and make a cheerful but specific announcement: "Dad has a wonderful new job in Los Angeles and we're going to move there in June. Now, how do you kids feel about it?"

Note carefully: you're only asking *how they feel about it,* not for a show of hands on whether or not you move. That decision must be made by the parents.

We've come across parents who, after having accepted the transfer, reneged because, they said, "Jennifer can't leave her ballet class," or "Eric can't bear being separated from his Grandma."

In such cases it's possible to work out a solution for Jennifer's fairly minor problem or Eric's more deep-seated one. But usually when an adult announces that the family can't move because his child is opposed to it, it's a fairly good guess that this adult is using little Eric or little Jennifer as a not very convincing excuse. It's the parent who doesn't want to move. And that's another story.

Back to your family conference. In this composite family, the members are, besides Mother and Father, Eric, aged six, Jennifer, aged eleven, and Bill, aged fifteen.

The announcement can precipitate loud wails of protest, shouts of joy, dead silence, or any of the above, depending on the temperament of each child.

In our scenario, Jennifer, the outgoing eleven-year-old and prima donna of the family, immediately sets up a wail of protest.

JENNIFER: *Mother!* I can't move! I just started ballet lessons! And besides, there's school, and all my friends . . .

BILL: Oh shut up, Jennifer! You can take ballet lessons in L.A. And maybe we can get you in the movies. Besides, if by friends you mean Peter Frank, aren't you maybe a little young for him? [Jennifer sticks out her tongue.] I don't think moving is a bad idea. I mean, I don't like leaving Chicago any more than anyone else, but if

> we moved to L.A., I could start taking courses at
> UCLA.
FATHER: Good for you, son!
MOTHER: Wait a minute, we haven't heard from Eric.
Eric, how do you *feel* about moving?
ERIC: Where's Los Angeles?

After a short break to explain to Eric where Los Angeles is, the family continues the discussion.

The purpose of the initial family conference is to let the children know that their interests are being considered in the impending move, and to give the parents a reading on what those interest are.

If the above scenario sounds like a rerun of the "Brady Bunch," a minimum risk family—the serious college-bound teen-ager, the frivolous but persuadable daughter and the innocent six year old—it's nevertheless from real life. So is the next one.

NOT UNLESS GRANDMA GOES TOO!

In this one, the children are a year older. After Mother makes the announcement, the first protest comes from sixteen-year-old Bill.

"I'm not going!" he says. "You can go move to Los Angeles with your swimming pool and all, but I like it here. I'm tired of being moved all over the place! I've got my job, I've got my friends."

JENNIFER: If you mean Sue Ellen Parsons, she can't stand you.
BILL: Oh, shut up, Jennifer! What do you know?
JENNIFER: A lot! Besides, I *would* like to move. Personally, I can't stand this boring place any longer. The

schools are terrible and the kids are just dull, dull, dull.

BILL: Just because Miss Roberts is failing you in social studies, and Peter Frank won't go out with you!

JENNIFER: Bill, you're really a rotten person!

MOTHER: Now, we haven't heard from Eric. Eric, what do you think about moving?

ERIC: If we go to Los Angeles, can I have a surfboard?

MOTHER: Well, not right away. Maybe when you're older.

ERIC: Then I'm not going unless Grandma goes with us!

What's happening here? What's more important is what isn't happening. True, the kids are protesting the move. They're squabbling and bickering among themselves, raising issues that may vanish when the child concerned gets a good grade or makes a new friend. And they're hardly proceeding according to *Roberts Rules of Order*.

What they're *not* doing is retreating into their private worlds and nursing their grievances, real or imagined, thereby magnifying the importance of their beefs in their own minds and mixing up issues that are connected with the move with issues that are not.

Getting all the issues out on the table is a good idea in the United Nations and an even better one in the united family.

WHERE DO WE GO FROM HERE?

But, you may ask, does the family conference *solve* anything? This type of meeting may initially seem a little chaotic, produce a lot of heat and bickering and very little light. But don't consider this a negative factor. Letting off steam will prevent the kids from holding in feelings and fears about relocating so that these feelings cannot be resolved. Of course

they can't resolve them right away, that is. The conference
does accomplish three things:
1. It makes children aware that they're a part of the up-
   rooting process, not household goods to be packed along
   with the china.
2. It gives them a chance to let off steam that might otherwise build up and explode later with disastrous results.
   The fighting and bickering that often erupt at such a
   gathering can drive parents up the wall. Yet in all this
   steam the kids are, whether or not they realize it, helping solve each other's problems. (In the sixties and early
   seventies, a very fashionable form of psychotherapy was
   the T-group or encounter group. These groups demon-
   strated how valuable it is for people to come together to
   express their feelings and thoughts freely so they can
   resolve concerns and problems. In a family conference
   on a sensitive issue you're running the ideal, do-it-
   yourself encounter or rap group).
3. It makes parents aware, by listening to the arguments
   and counter arguments, of what's going on with the kids.
   They'll pick up plenty of clues so they can deal intelli-
   gently with their children's feelings and practical problems.

The focus of this chapter is your concern about your child.
While in most cases your concerns run well beyond the desirable limits, parents can use as much help as they can get
to avoid guilt and gather information.

How can we predict whether a child might be easy or difficult to move? We'd like to convince you, first, that if a child
has done something once, the probability is very high that
he or she can do it again. If your daughter made friends
where you are, you can make money by betting she'll do it
again in her new home. If your son was accepted as a good
athlete he'll attain the same recognition in his next community. All they need is your support and understanding.

Here is The Children's Relocation Predictor that shows

what to assess about your child. It should predict any unusual problems.

For each trait listed, rate your child's ability as acceptable or unacceptable. For the areas rated unacceptable, look closely at the next section, which discusses possible difficulties that may develop after a move and some techniques to deal with them.

CHILDREN'S RELOCATION PREDICTOR

	Acceptable	Unacceptable
School grades		
Making friends		
Relates well in new situations		
Adventurous		
Flexible (reaction to change in plans)		
Can occupy self		
Has varied interests		
Will tell parents if something bothering him		
Amount of time child wants to be by self		
Belongs to groups		
Plays well with other chlidren		
Frequency of minor ailments		

ANALYSIS OF TRAITS

School Grades

A child who has trouble with grades will most often continue to have some difficulty in the new location and school system. It's most important to gain the clearest possible understanding of *why* the child is having academic trouble so the best approach and program can be developed in the new school system. When a child has had academic problems the school can often evaluate the child's functioning and develop a specific remedial program. Parents frequently worry that communicating a child's past problems to the new school will result in stereotyping the child and create a bias. In our experience there is much more to be gained than lost from a frank discussion with the new principal and other school personnel, who will be working with your child. This is best followed up by sending any school records, evaluations or remedial program materials to the new school.

A word of caution: it's easy for a relocated family whose child has had academic problems to blame problems on the school in the old community. This can lead to ignoring the child's problem to his detriment. Don't let this happen to you!

Making Friends

The best predictor of a child's ability to make friends in a new community is his prior pattern of friendships. A child who has been somewhat of a loner and has difficulties in forming friendships will need a lot of support and help in the new community. Take the time to talk to your child about what it's going to feel like to make new friends. Don't be afraid to share your own concerns and anxieties about making friends. Help your child work out some specific ways for meeting people.

With children who are slow to make friends it's critical to make sure they immediately get involved in the activities that interest them. Sign them up for little league, soccer, summer camp, etc., *before* you move. We've heard from too many parents, "When we got there it was too late to sign up." Caution: don't expect your child to have a new set of friends in one month; it takes time. Don't mistake the normal adjustment process for an indication that your child will not make friends.

Relates Well in New Situations

Some children are slower than others to warm up to new situations. On the first day of school, Johnny may run onto the playground and join a group of children while Robert may stand around and get the lay of the land before he decides to join a group. One is not better or healthier; they're simply different styles of functioning. If your child is a Robert he's apt to adjust more slowly and express more anxiety about the move.

Prior to the move allow him to express his fears; listen, empathize and don't try to talk him out of his feelings. Maintain an attitude that you're confident he'll be able to adjust. Many parents with a Robert panic when he adjusts to the new community in the same way he's adjusted to everything else— slowly.

Adventurous

The child who is not adventurous will initially need a lot of parental support in making contacts outside of the home. Try to make the scouting of the neighborhood and community a family affair; don't push him out the door the first day and say "go play with the kids on the block." Meet the neighbors together and go to new places as a family.

Flexible

The child who does not react well to changes in plans is likely to experience a lot of anxiety in the days just prior to moving, on moving day and in the first week after the move.

Understand that the need for order and predictability is probably one way this child has of dealing with the worries of moving to a new community.

For this child it's important to provide as much predictability as possible. Take the time to explain when you'll pack, when the movers will come, how long it takes to get from Chicago to Dallas. If changes in the family schedule arise, try to let such a child know about them as far in advance as you can. This child is likely to get pretty uptight when the movers start packing his belongings and they're no longer in "the right place." Reassure the child that they've been carefully packed and labeled and will go right into his room in Dallas.

Sometimes a child with this style will get so focused on the disruptions in schedule and the relocation disorder that other anxieties about moving get lost. After the move when things have calmed down, take time out to talk about any concerns that got lost in heat of the move. Do not wait until after you've moved to find that there's no little league or opportunity to take modern dance. A child with few interests will need to feel quickly there are equivalents in the new community or he might quickly get discouraged.

Can Occupy Self

A child who has difficulty occupying himself and needs a lot of direction is likely to find it difficult to get into activities and interests in a new community. You will have to be very active in making sure you find organizations and activities that are equivalent to what the child is accustomed.

This type of child is also likely to find the moving period stressful because you have less time to spend with him. It might be helpful to explain exactly why, in the days just prior to and following the move, mommy and daddy will be very busy and will have less available time. Help this child plan some things he can do to keep busy.

Has Varied Interests

For the child with a narrow range of interests, it is crucial to research the new community thoroughly in advance. Do not wait until after you've moved to find that there's no Little League or modern dance class. A child with few interests will need to feel quickly that interesting activities await him in the new community or he might quickly get discouraged.

Will Tell Parents If Something Is Bothering Him

For a child who tends to keep worries and feelings to himself, the concern is that you will not find out about a relocation-related difficulty until it has become a full blown problem. If your child fits this description, make sure that you are verbal about difficulties, day to day feelings and adjustment tasks *you* face. Talk about these things at meals, family gatherings or schedule regular family conferences to help each other out with the move. Such children often think that a problem or feeling is something to be ashamed of (or indicates weakness). They need parental assurance that their feelings, worries and day to day adjustment problems don't mean something "bad" about them. The example you set will help them best.

Amount of Time Child Wants to Spend Alone

A child who can spend little time alone may find the time right after the move quite difficult. These children, who are very social, or like to be with other people, are often very sensitive to feelings of rejection and loneliness. Sometimes a child like this can be exasperating when parents feel pressured and overburdened. Try to be patient especially when you can't make sure this child understands your tenseness and that you're not being rejecting. Include this child in a lot of family activities right after the move.

Belongs to Groups

Groups provide a good way for a child to identify with (and get involved in) a new setting. They're an important help for a positive relocation experience. The parents with a child who tends not to be a joiner need to look for other ways to help the child identify with the area. For this child, learning the history of the town or state, going to sites of special interest and importance, rooting for local sports teams are all helpful in fostering some geographic identification.

Plays Well with Other Children

The child who does not play well with other children can be expected to have some difficulty making friends in the neighborhood and at school. Under the tension of a move and meeting new children, interpersonal difficulties tend to become magnified.

With this child, it's important to have specific discussions about initial contacts with other children. If you pick up some things your child sometimes says or does to turn off other kids, try gently to help your child understand this. You might even want to role play these situations with your child to help him find some effective ways of meeting other children.

Frequency of Minor Ailments

The child who is prone to minor ailments is often a sensitive youngster who has difficulty talking about his feelings to others. This child can be expected to experience a good deal of stress after a move and will probably go through a period of many minor ailments. You want to give such a child every opportunity to express all concerns. These children, however, sometimes use the ailments as an escape mechanism—from school, from meeting new people or from other tension producing situations. Be careful not to allow this; be supportive but firm so your child does not miss so much school and avoid people for so long that he'll really get behind the eight ball.

WHAT HAPPENS AFTER THE CONFERENCE?

The parents, individually or separately, had best start heart-to-heart talks with the children, pursuing further the grievances raised in the family conference.

Some parents find this difficult.

"What," demanded John Taylor, "am I supposed to *tell* a teen-age boy who won't leave his high school because he's finally made the football team? Hell, I mean, he doesn't make any damned sense! Last year, he wanted to be a doctor. This year, he wants to be a pro ball player, for crying out loud! Doctor maybe; pro ball player—no way! But how do I *tell* him without breaking his heart?"

"And what," demanded his wife Elaine, "am I supposed to tell a nine-year-old girl who must leave her girl friends? I know she'll make new ones wherever we go, but she doesn't know this. She couldn't. When I tell her that she'll forget Susie and Jane a few months after the move, she cries."

The answer to these understandable parent complaints is ridiculously simple.

You don't *tell* them anything. Nothing.

That's right: nothing!

You listen, and listen and listen and then you listen some more.

Fight the inevitable temptation to lay on them the benefits

of your experience. They'll consider this irrelevant, just as you did when you were young, remember? Every time you're tempted to say "you're all wrong" and come up with some marvelous advice, substitute, "Why do you think that?"

You may be surprised at what *you* learn.

Parents are used to telling children what to do: eat your breakfast! take your medicine! And how to do it: hit a ball, bake a cake.

But no one can *tell* a child (or a person of any age) how to *feel*. It simply cannot be done. It's like fighting the law of gravity. Parents who try only compound the problem. If children are given enough breathing room and rope, they will (except for the truly disturbed) climb to emotional safety by themselves. Every time. Every psychologist knows this from professional experience.

MEET THE WITCH DOCTOR

Mrs. Carrie Vincent, a high-spirited grandmother of seventy-six, is regarded with awe by her children. "I think Grandma Vincent is some sort of witch doctor," her daughter-in-law, Ruth, confided to a friend. "Whenever any of our kids has a problem, we tell him, 'go talk to Grandma.' Like last week, Ralph was all upset about which college to choose. I couldn't help him, I don't know enough about the schools involved. So he went and talked to Grandma. When he came back, he had resolved the problem. I don't know how she does it."

Grandma knows, but she never got around to sharing her trade secrets with her children.

"It's really very easy," she told us with a sly smile. "I just sit there and let the kids talk away. Pretty soon they have it all figured out for themselves. I've always known how to do this. And now I'm told that young fellows like yourselves are making maybe $25 an hour doing it."

More than that, Grandma, a whole lot more.

The Vincent family is extraordinarily blessed by having a matriarch who can fill in for a professional counselor and help resolve everyday problems.

Grandma does not have a string of degrees behind her name. In fact, she did not quite finish high school. But she knows instinctively and from shrewd observation that the thing to do when people bring their problems to you is not to talk but to listen.

If Grandma can do it, you can, too.

Sometimes, as in the case of Ralph's choice of colleges, the problem can be resolved quickly. At other times, where a child's problems are continuing problems—difficulties in school, problems with friends or fears and anxieties about moving—it takes a little longer. Let it.

For what the temporarily distressed child needs, more than advice, is another person whom he trusts, who says, "Tell me about it. Whatever it is, I'm here, I'm with you, and I love you."

That shouldn't be hard for any parent to say.

WHAT ABOUT OLDER TEENS?

A fair question. High school juniors and seniors sometimes have more than emotional ties to their present location. Phil, who must complete his present course of studies for college admission; Marcia, whose summer job in a state senator's office is going to mean a lot on her resumé *after* she gets her B.A.; or Ken, a football or basketball star who stands a good chance of an athletic scholarship, have valid reasons for not moving with their parents.

For these young adults (and that's what they are, *young adults*), the possibility of staying behind and boarding with a relative or friend or even living in a furnished room of their own should be thoroughly discussed in their individual conferences with parents. It often proves to be the best thing.

Phil, Marcia and Ken will be off to college in a year or so anyway. It's best to look on a slightly premature separation from the family unit as a trial run at independence.

What if you're worried that separation from the family might just turn them toward loose living, drug or alcohol addiction, or worse? You'd be wrong 99 percent of the time. Youngsters, whose objections to moving are seriously career-oriented, are not likely to throw away these ambitions simply because they're away from their parents. If they want to stay, need to stay and seem to know why they need to stay, then this is an alternative that can be seriously considered. It's not an easy or simple decision, and we certainly understand the anxiety this decision produces.

We'd encourage a professional consultation where doubt exists. Parents would do well to combine information from school, clergyman, guidance counselor, physician and perhaps local psychologist. Parents must get over the idea that a child's wish to stay represents a rejection of them or that they might be "abandoning" a child. Staying behind can sometimes be a mature, legitimate request.

Some situations require very difficult decisions from parents and generate great family turmoil. Leaving behind a teen-ager who is still in high school is not easy for most people and some youngsters make it an impossible dilemma, not to mention young people who do get involved with drugs, drinking or get into trouble with the law.

BART REFUSED TO LEAVE

Sam and Violet Shuster lived in a small, southwestern town and were faced with a transfer to Mexico for a three year tour with guaranteed repatriation to corporate headquarters in New York. The assignment was most attractive to Sam but their sixteen-year-old son, Bart, refused to leave his friends.

The family had moved to their present town when Bart

was thirteen. It was his first move. Overnight, he ceased acting like a little boy playing with toy cars and models and expected to be treated like a twenty-one-year-old. Bart chose his school's most notorious failures as friends. His grades soon dropped to barely passing. Talk of college turned to talk of motorcycle racing, and he put down anyone who valued education. The parents were sure he used drugs and was involved in some stealing.

This family consulted us about their dilemma and were, understandably, in an anxious state. They certainly had a problem that should have been faced before, but now the relocation confronted them with an emergency; Bart was out of control and they could not force him to go with them. "He'd surely just run away" said Violet Shuster. "I've just about decided to accept limiting my career, turn down the opportunity and stay here so at least we can keep an eye on him," her husband added.

Sam Shuster had to be confronted with unhappy facts: his solution was another way to avoid helping Bart; the father's resentment of the son would probably live on for years and further alienate Bart. Our advice was to get Bart into a teenage therapeutic school and accept the transfer. A good institution was recommended in Texas so that visits could be made easily.

This case demonstrates how a relocation decision can sometimes be used unknowingly to avoid other painful issues. Without counseling, our guess is that Sam Shuster would have turned down the assignment and Bart would be without help today. A follow-up about one year later showed that Bart is doing well at the school and will probably join his parents in Mexico. He is eager to do so.

It's also useful to understand what happened to Bart when he moved at age thirteen. Bart was somewhat immature for his age when the family moved, but in upstate New York he had made friends with boys much like himself. He was not ready for the more mature group of emerging teen-agers but that was okay; he was safe because he had his own group for security.

The Shuster's felt that Bart made the move easily. "He didn't seem to miss his friends, never mentioned Clarksville, and really didn't protest the move at all," Mrs. Shuster told us.

In retrospect, the boy's immaturity should have been interpreted as the first clue, not of emotional problems, but of the effect a move might have on Bart and what support he needed from his parents. The second clue calling for some parental intervention was the quiescence of this thirteen-year-old—again a signal that he needed to be encouraged to shape and voice his feelings about the move. He must have felt very bad about leaving his pals.

It happens to many parents, but the Shusters should have exercised more control during the first few critical weeks after the move. They left an immature Bart so that he *had* to prove himself something he was not.

Parents in this situation should not be afraid to direct a child and place limits on friendships until the child gets over his shock and his urgent need to be accepted immediately.

GETTING READY TO ROLL

Individual problems aside, there are many practical measures any family can take not only to lessen the traumas of relocation, but make an *adventure* of it.

Learn all you can about the new location. Subscribe to the local paper immediately, but don't stop there. Write to the chamber of commerce for promotional material on the town's future, to the county historical society for material on its past. If the new location is in any way a tourist attraction or there is one nearby, most travel agents can get you booklets on the scenic wonders and other attractions, all in glorious color and suitable for pinning up on the family bulletin board.

Visit your public library and take out books on the town, city or general area you're headed for: lavish books on the New England heritage if you're moving to West Hartford; tales of the old west if it's Wherever, Wyoming.

Secret: There is no such place as Dullsville, U.S.A. There just ain't! Dramatizing New York, Los Angeles, San Francisco or Boston is easy. In some cases you may even have to put some of the big name cities into perspective, pointing out that New York isn't wall-to-wall discotheques, the West Coast is not populated entirely by surfers and movie stars.

Less glamorous cities obviously aren't as easy to romance.

Pittsburgh doesn't sound very exciting, but if your kids aren't intrigued by the daring of the robber barons, start them rooting right away for the Steelers.

Really small towns present a problem, but nothing's impossible. If it's Two Trees, Texas, you have the whole panorama of the Lone Star State to work with. If it's Who Knows, West Virginia, that's where the Waltons come from. And if it's Forget It, Florida, how many miles to Disney World?

If your children are bookworms, you're in luck. One small girl was very negative about a move to Newton, Massachusetts (despite the excellent schools) until her mother told her that their house would be only a ten minute drive from the Alcott house where her beloved Little Women—Meg, Jo, Beth and Amy—grew up.

A mother whose descriptions of the flourishing commerce of Atlanta, Georgia and its fine restaurants and hotels made no impression on her daughter confided somewhat guiltily, "I finally bought her *Gone with the Wind* in paperback and that did it. Did I do wrong?"

No Way!

TV can be useful to help portray an area to children. Be alert to any documentaries or shows that might offer a good picture of the state or city you're moving to. (Frequently, the cameras at sports events scan the area prior to a game or during intermission).

HOW MAPS HELP

Maps are effective too. Showing, telling, reading and watching programs can provide the atmosphere; a map superimposes the geographical reality, the physical shape of home to come.

When the move is settled on, post a large map of the United States on a convenient wall. Place a colored pushpin on the town where you live now. Situate another colored pushpin on the new location. This can give even a five-year-old something to think about. The next step is a detailed map of the area with pushpins inserted at points of interest.

If the breadwinner of the family has to make a number of side trips and be absent from his family in the course of relocation, the map game turns into "Where is Daddy Now?" with pushpins to chart his course.

For the frequently moved family, the mounted map can become a family treasure.

When teen-aged Chuck Simpson, a veteran of many moves, told his new friends he had been "all over the map" he could prove it. His mom and dad had saved the moving map, just as some families save the family Bible. And there it all was. Shades of Lewis and Clark!

Before this turns into a travelogue, let's nail down the main points.

1. A show, tell and study program for children not only increases enthusiasm for the move, but it adds substantially to a child's basic information and ability to evaluate that information constructively and in relatively good cheer.

2. Such a program does the same for the parents. If you're forced to be a teacher, then you've got to be a student, too. One woman we know who moved her family several times in the United States (and a few times overseas) turned her experience to terrific use; she's trying to write historical romances. Don't count on that happening to you. But opening doors for your children can often open doors for you.

3. Be careful that the material you present is what interests the child and isn't foisting your interests on him.

4. This is also the beginning of the identification with the new place before he gets there. If you want your child to grow roots, this is a way of starting the seeds in a hothouse before putting them out in the garden at the mercy of the elements.

MAKING THE MOST OF THE PRELIMINARY TRIP

Nearly all companies underwrite expenses for a preliminary trip to the new location. Customarily, the family wage earner makes this trip alone, selects housing alone, and reports back to the family with a polaroid of the new house and a general description of the area.

The better way—the whole family goes. You may have to spend a little of your own money above the company allowance, but it's worth it. The trip can be turned into an adventure. As a family, you can visit restaurants, go sightseeing, discover what the town has to offer in the way of shopping, museums, theater and sports. If there are friends, acquaintances or approachable company people in town, visit them to get a firsthand feel of the place. In any town, you're bound to find something *someone* is enthusiastic about.

For example, Jack Johnson made his first visit to Out There, Idaho, alone. His report: terrific golf course, good steak house, and Charlie Anderson lives there.

This made little or no impression on his non-golfing wife Lily; his older daughter Betsy, the budding actress; his younger daughter Amy, the bird watcher; or his son Patrick, the Little League ball player.

On the second visit, the family went as a group. Betsy, who couldn't care less about golf courses and steak houses, discovered immediately that there was an active little theatre group that accepted summer apprentices. Amy couldn't understand why her father hadn't told her about the natural history museum in a nearby university town. Patrick discovered that there was Little League ball in the new location, too; besides, the kids were big on ice hockey. And Lily discovered that not only was Charlie Anderson's wife a bridge enthusiast but shared her passion for gourmet cooking.

This is more than social pleasantry. It's emotional solace.

Having something tangible to look forward to greatly lessens the pangs of separation. It also reduces the deepest fears of the relocating family—the fear of the unknown just because it is unknown.

Finances may not allow every family to make an exploratory visit as a group. If this is true for you, some paper work is in order.

Let each family member make a list detailing his or her extra special interest. It's simply a matter of each member of the family WRITING DOWN what he or she would like to find in the new location and handing the sheets to father.

Has he heard it all before? Probably. Has it registered? Maybe, maybe not. So writing it down is important.

But the head of household who goes forth to scout the new territory with a notebook to remind him that his wife *really* wants to know about clothes shopping, his daughter cares desperately about ballet lessons, and his son hopes to join a rock group can research these matters.

He may not find what everybody wants. But he can report on what there is. And the family will know he tried.

HOW TO SAY FAREWELL

As moving time approaches, make it easy for children to say their goodbyes.

Children, even as adults, are loath to leave their friends and even more loath to admit it. If you hear Jackie saying of his best friend, Allen, "I don't want to play with *him* any more, he's *dumb*," don't believe a word of it.

What Jackie is really doing is verbalizing a bit of eight-year-old bravado. He is going to lose Allen, so he is minimizing the loss by deciding Allen is dumb anyway.

Don't argue. Act.

First of all, be very open about the move with your children's friends: "Jackie's daddy has a new job in Chicago, and we *have* to move. We're sure going to miss White Plains—and especially you."

You can say it. Jackie probably can't.

Having said it, don't press the point. Do invite Allen and your other children's friends to see pictures of the new house and the new location and promote the idea that they and their parents will be visiting there someday. (Here you're treading a delicate line. If you're close friends with the parents, you're safe. If not, don't promise other people's children more than you can deliver.)

What you can deliver is a bang-up going away party for your kids and their friends. For little ones, it may be an ice cream and cake bon voyage with paper hats. For in-betweens, a girls' lunch and movie or a boys' party to witness a sporting event with tickets and hot dogs supplied by Dad. For teens it could be a disco party in the basement. For all ages, it could be a family picnic or cookout thrown by your family. It's not the style that counts, it's the message—you're really our friends and we're really going to miss you.

If this is all too much for you (and it may well be, considering the other pressures of moving) perhaps a close friend or relative might do it for you. A kid's event is a kid's event whether it's sponsored by you, Aunt Maggie, Uncle Ed, or even Allen's parents.

On a one-to-one level, explain to your kids that even if they are moving away from Allen or Mary Sue or whomever, they can still write. Separation doesn't mean loss of friends. Don't you still write to your sister, Lorena, or your old college friend, Lillian, even though you're miles apart? Doesn't Daddy still see Uncle Arthur, his high school buddy? Chances are the kids know Lorena, Lillian and Arthur, who still come to visit. Explain to them that their real friends will stay friends in later life, too.

Encourage them to write. Permit phone calls within reason.

What about the little kids who can't write? The best solution we know is the parent supervised postcard campaign.

If five-year-old Priscilla is desolate at leaving her friend Abby, promise her that you and she will write together. Buy up a stock of postcards at the new location and every week help Priscilla to send one to Abby. "This is a lake near where we live, Love, Priscilla" will do, no matter who writes or prints it.

Probably, in fact almost always, within a few months Priscilla will have found new friends and forgotten Abby. It happens that way at five and six. At that time, the postcard ritual can taper off. It has served its purpose.

SECURITY MEASURES

Children, even as adults, dislike leaving their friends. And even as adults dislike leaving familiar surroundings or abandoning their possessions.

A temptation of many parents, who wouldn't consider moving without taking along the stereo system or Grandma's china, can be very callous about children's possessions, which seem like, and often are, a bunch of junk.

A battered doll, a collection of baseball cards or comic books or a pinup picture of Baryshnikov may be junk, but these possessions are your children's junk and thus to be valued.

When moving time approaches, tell each of the children to gather together their most prized possessions and pack or pile them. From a teen-age girl, you may get a carefully filed set of press clippings and photographs, from a small child, a junk box full of toys and totems. Whatever the stuff is, make clear to your youngsters that all they value goes with you—so get it together.

LEAVING YOUR FRIENDS WITHOUT LOSING THEM

Leaving a community where you've been happy is always hard. But some families make it a lot harder on themselves (and their friends) than they need to.

Marge and Hal Norton were genuinely sorry to leave Lakeville, where they had lived for five years. Their solution was to tough it out.

"I believe in the clean break," Marge told us. "As soon as we knew we were moving, we decided to act in our own minds as if we had moved already. We put all of our energies into packing and planning for the new life. Oh, sure, we let it be known we were moving, but we sort of stopped seeing people. I mean, we didn't want any weepy scenes or any of that stuff with people I may never see again. I can't stand mushy good-byes. Besides, as Satchel Paige said, 'Don't look back, something may be gaining on you,' right?"

Wrong.

The clean break theory is all very well for Humphrey Bogart and Ingrid Bergman in *Casablanca,* but it's a little melodramatic for a family moving a long-distance phone call away from friends they have cherished. Besides, when Marge and Hal decamped silently, leaving only a forwarding address, their friends were hurt and puzzled. What did they do to deserve this?

A CASE OF SOUR GRAPES

Mel and Tillie Thompson were equally unhappy about leaving Lakeville, but they chose to cry sour grapes. "Actually, it's the best thing," Tillie told friends. "We never were happy here: the schools are awful, there's no place to swim, and the winters are brutal. Of course we'll miss our friends, but . . ."

Did the friends believe this? yes, except the part about being missed. Tillie was putting down their town, and, by extension, putting them down as well. By the time the Thompsons moved, nobody was interested in any farewell parties or good-bye scenes, mushy or otherwise.

WITH THEIR NOSES IN THE AIR

Ed and Edna Connors took still another tack. "It's really a great opportunity for Ed," Edna announced. "I mean, it's sort of a lateral move, but it puts him right in line for personnel director, and I don't have to tell you what *that* means.

"And of course, since it's the main office, we'll be socializing with all the brass. Ed will probably kill me, but I'm buying a whole new wardrobe."

Ed and Edna's friends were truly happy for them. They got together and threw a bang-up farewell party. It began with a few perfunctory toasts to the old gang and good times past, and progressed to toasts, becoming increasingly more verbose, to Ed and Edna, their new success, and their new life. There were presents. Funny ones: a T-shirt for Ed, imprinted with the words "Chairman of the Bored" and real ones: a sterling silver sugar and creamer for entertaining executive wives at tea. Everybody had a terrific time.

The day after the party, a sleepy Edna said to her equally sleepy husband, "What a great party! They really love us in Lakeville." And Ed replied, "You know it! Why shouldn't they? It's nice to know you have such good and loyal friends."

Four houses down the block, a morning dialogue was going on between the Connors's good friends Dottie and Dan Turner.

DAN: Well, there go Ed and Edna.
DOTTIE: Yeah. I'm really happy for them. I must write Edna—I mean, maybe they'll come back and visit or we could visit them.
DAN: Forget it, Dottie! Ed's a big man in his company now, and, as Edna said, they'll be socializing with the brass. They're too important for us now.

WHO NEEDS FRIENDS, ANYWAY?

What mistake did all these couples make? In leaving Lakeville, all three families managed, consciously or unconsciously, to divest themselves of the friends they had made there. Perhaps permanently. Too bad. And so unnecessary.

Everybody needs friends. We're not tied to friends by kinship and legal obligation, as we are to parents, children and mates, but we need friends just the same. Children need other children, adults need other adults, whether they're married or single, a few friends that are really close plus a wider circle of good acquaintances.

Happy families need friends. Unhappy families, split asunder by death, divorce or the inevitable fact of children growing up and moving out need them even more.

Isn't this obvious? Of course! It doesn't take a Ph.D. in psychology to know what friends are for. We all grew up on books, movies, soap operas and popular song lyrics that placed true friendship second only to true love.

Then why are we spelling all this out all over again? Because it needs to be spelled out over and over again to individuals and couples on the move who believe (or say they believe) that they're a breed apart, that for them, friends are expendable.

We hear a variety of explanations:
1. I (we) don't have time to make friends. We move around too much.
2. I (we) don't need friends. Fred's (my) career is what counts; and getting involved with people would only tie us down.
3. We need friends—but having each other is more important.
4. I (we) don't want to make friends. We did once and had to leave them. I don't want to be hurt again.
5. Or, any combination of the above.

Next come the self-proclaimed loners. They fall roughly into three categories. (See if you recognize anyone you know.)

THE LONE RANGER

This is usually a man, though more and more frequently these days it can be a woman, too. Chuck Somerville is a good example. "Hanging around with your high school buddies or college friends," Chuck told us, "is okay for guys who're stuck in one town or one job. But I can't afford it. My world is my job and the company. That's where the action is, where the bucks are. For me, that's also where the satisfaction is. I don't even like to get too close to other guys in the company. I mean, supposing I get promoted? What happens then? Like they say, 'he travels fastest who travels alone.' "

Chuck is divorced, which is not surprising. Not too many women are crazy about being Tonto.

THE TWO MUSKETEERS

These are the togetherness kids, the devoted married partners who reason that, through thick and thin, they've always got each other. Connie Kellman puts it this way: "When I married Bernie I knew we'd be moving every three or four years. I decided, and it was a conscious decision—we talked it all out—that we wouldn't expect to have friends. After all, we've got each other, and that's got to be it, for us."

Connie is pregnant. What, we asked her, about the third musketeer? Connie looked puzzled. "Well," she said, "he or she is just going to have to learn to live the way we do. All for one and one for all. It's not the worst life for a kid."

That's what *she* thinks.

THE EMBITTERED ONE

We usually hear this from a woman, but only because men are less likely to admit to these feelings.

Penny and Jay Paul have moved six times in thirteen years. Penny is in charge of social life, and at the Pauls house there is a minimum of social life. "I finally got smart," Penny says. "We made a lot of good friends in the first town we lived in. Then we had to leave them and it hurt a lot. The same thing happened in the second town. I'm not making the same mistake again. 'Don't get involved' is my motto. If you don't make friends in the first place, you can't be hurt when you lose them."

It's all so plausible. And all so wrong.

MOVING MEANS MORE FRIENDS, NOT FEWER

Many mobile people, including those profiled here, believe that because they don't have a handy, built-in set of permanent friends and acquaintances as stay-at-homes do, they're inevitably destined to forgo friendship entirely. It follows, according to their reasoning (or defensive reactions) that they don't need or can't afford or don't want friends, anyway, *so there*!

They've got it backwards in every possible way. Let's try to untangle their tangle.

Mobile individuals and families need and want friends (real friends) as much as, if not more, than those who do not move. But they seem to be at a disadvantage. The non-mobile families can sometimes neglect friends, ignore them, get in fights with them, but usually pick up with them again, because there they are, right down the block; they come with the territory.

But every town isn't Waltons' Mountain. Sometimes it's Peyton Place. Plenty of people, who are not in position to move, envy the movers the opportunity to meet new, different and presumably exciting people.

And if you're still yearning for the simple life in the old hometown, maybe you'd better take another look at the place. Many non-mobile people who planned to live out their life in Plainsville, as their parents and grandparents did, are discovering that Plainsville is moving away from them. The older generation has died off, industries have moved in, bringing new people along with them. Highways are being built, shopping centers are going up alongside them. What ever did happen to Main Street? Presto: many would-be non-mobiles are finding themselves strangers on their own turf.

The career-oriented Lone Rangers can afford friends without jeopardizing their careers. Charlie Somerville (and this is true also of his female counterpart) is reluctant to form close ties within the company, and this makes sense. In a working group, whether its a big corporation, a military unit, or the cast of a musical comedy, the group goal is what counts. If Charlie is to be effective in the group, he often can't afford close personal ties that might diminish this effectiveness. (Who can fire his best friend?) Charlie puts this in terms of "getting ahead," which doesn't sound overly attractive. But wait; he's talking mostly about doing his job, and that's fine.

This is not to say that Charlie can't have friends outside the company. In any location he's moved to, Charlie can join jogging groups, play tennis, get involved in once a week poker or political discussion groups, whatever suits his fancy. If he's reasonably high up in his company, he's a shoo-in for lecturing in adult education courses at the local community college on business administration, bookkeeping, business English or whatever. The pay is minimal but the satisfaction can be great.

This kind of leisure-time activity is *not* going to make Charlie any money or advance his career directly. What it can do is provide him with a healthy and challenging life and maybe some new options. In the pursuit of leisure activities, Charlie can meet and hopefully make friends with a wide range of people he'd never meet at work—professors, physicians, lawyers, politicians, executives in other industries. Windows on worlds he's never experienced.

The businessmen from other companies might just turn out to yield fortuitous friendships, mighty useful for the time when Charlie might decide to change jobs.

The Charlie Somervilles of this world cannot only afford to make friends—they can't afford not to—any more than can those who have no job related cop out but don't bother to make friends because they have their family or fear making friends because of the pain of loss. Denying yourself the pleasures of friends, whatever rationale you use, may work in the present, but in the future it can only lead to a lonely old age (couples can be lonely, too) with few precious and dimming memories to hark back to.

WHAT FRIENDS ARE FOR

Friends are for fun. Friends are for companionship—people to do things with, discuss ideas with, compare notes with on life's joys and heartaches. Friends are for support when we need it.

On a deeper level, those friends we're really close to become in a way part of us. We *incorporate* them—that is, we absorb and to a degree sometimes adopt their attitudes, their ways of doing things, their outlooks on life. And they adopt ours. We are changed by good friends—for better or worse.

The quickest way to come to grips with this concept is to think of your parents.

Parents are our first best friends. In infancy and early childhood we have no choice but to incorporate their values, attitudes, ways of doing things.

How many times have you heard the old clichés? "She's her mother all over again." "He's a chip off the old block."

Most behavior patterns, mind-sets, manners, even mannerisms are transmitted by parents to the next generation.

As we grow older, we make new alliances, especially with teachers and with peers. Most of us can remember at least one special teacher or friend who made a lifelong impression. A biochemist told us, "Mr. Hunsaker taught general science at the sixth grade level. But it was the *way he talked about science* that started me on my career. He's retired now, but I still go back and visit him when I feel I need some words of wisdom."

A female personnel director said, "When I was in high school, I had one idea—to graduate and get married. My best friend, Mary Kate—I guess she was a premature women's libber—convinced me that I was college material, that I could have an education, a career *and* a husband.

"She changed my whole life. She says I changed hers, too, by showing her how to use makeup, and maybe I did. Anyway, even though I live in Boston and she lives in New Jersey, we're still on the phone all the time, and at least twice a year we visit back and forth with our families."

WHEN YOU'RE ON YOUR OWN

Okay, you may say, that goes for parents and teachers, school and college friends. But once out in the world, the buddy system doesn't work any more. But it does! And for adults, especially adults who move around a lot, it works even better.

Out in the world, you get to *choose* your own best buddies, after all. You're not restricted to family, teachers, classmates or whatever kids happen to live on your block.

Out in the world, as an adult with your own identity, you can pick your friends or wait for them to pick and choose you. No matter what your private image may be of yourself, your credentials as a business person or business couple give you instant cachet in the eyes of the citizens of your new home environment.

Small towns, whether the small town is New Vista, New Jersey (with the highest per capita income in the country) or Whistle Stop, Wisconsin (where they never heard of per capita income) are intensely interested in newcomers. Rich, poor or in between, most people want to make friends. Meet them halfway.

Where will it get you? Among the old line families of New Vista, you may meet another Mr. Hunsaker, this time in the guise of a retired executive in your own field. The corporate wife and/or professional woman is almost bound to meet a dozen variations of Mary Kate.

MAKING IT IN WHISTLE STOP

In Whistle Stop, Wisconsin, you are, realistically speaking, not likely to find too many of your business and professional opposite numbers. But in just such a town, Mike Marrone, a born New Yorker, joined a fishing club. He met Dave Dunning, owner of the local garage, who introduced him to what is now his lifelong hobby and passion—tinkering with and restoring antique cars. Although Mike has moved on, they still correspond and see each other at least twice a year at car rallies and auctions.

Mike's wife, Terry, joined the Ladies Aid Society of the Methodist Church, the only church in town. "Not," Terry confesses, "for religious reasons—I was brought up a good Italian Catholic—but for something to do."

The first thing the Ladies Aid ladies gave Terry to do was to bring a covered dish to the church fair. When her grandmother's lasagna won second prize, Terry was in. This is how Terry met Anni Swenson, wife of a dairy farmer. The two families clicked: the Swenson kids taught the Marrone kids how to ride horseback, and Terry, a former food writer, was able to give the Swensons's oldest daughter valuable tips on preparing for a career as a home economist.

Now that the Marrones have moved on, the relationship lasts. Terry and Anni write, the children keep up with each other. And an annual Marrone ritual, no matter where they're located, is a real old-fashioned farm vacation at the Swensons.

Terry and Mike's lives were changed, surely for the better, by making brand new friends in their early forties. Of course, serendipity is involved. Real friends or people with the potential to be real friends don't turn up every time you attend a block party or go to a meeting of the newcomers club. But if you don't make the effort in the first place, you can truly be certain that nothing will happen at all.

What have you got to lose? The worst that can happen is a wasted social evening. The best that can happen is meeting someone who may just turn out to be a valued, lifelong friend.

We've said it before, and we'll say again: people on the move have the opportunity to meet more, many more, potential friends than stay-at-homes. And those friendships can be nurtured and can grow, even though physical distance, as it must, intervenes. It all depends on the way you go about it.

HOW TO CULTIVATE YOUR GARDEN OF FRIENDSHIPS

Paradoxically, the first step toward keeping good friends is knowing how to lose them. Not to lose them entirely, but you must know how to keep the ties intact even though you're moving half a continent away; how to leave town and still take with you what was really valuable to you in that town (and we're not talking about your seashell collection or handmade quilts).

If you're leaving a community and you're genuinely sorry to be leaving, don't try to brave it out. Admit it! Tell those you've been close to how much you hate to leave even if the schools are terrible and the winters too cold.

This seemingly simple step is difficult for many people. Whatever their professed reasons, the real reasons are fear of the pain of loss for themselves (and their friends) and, oddly enough, fear of rejection, as well as a general disinclination to show emotion.

Phyllis Little couldn't bear to tell her best friend, Millie Sue, that she and Hal were leaving. "She'd cry and I'd cry and I couldn't take that." And so she did not tell Millie Sue, who, of course, heard about it through a third party. Two days before moving, Phyllis dropped by to bid the most casual of farewells to Millie Sue, who responded in kind. The two women, briefly best friends, never communicated again. A little crying, Phyllis realized long afterwards, would have been better. She sometimes thinks of writing to Millie

Sue, but after her cool farewell she can't think what to say.

Dottie James took another approach. "I certainly don't want to tell anyone we're sorry to leave Fullers Falls, especially Elaine and Steve Novak. They've been our closest friends for seven years since we've been here, and just the other night Elaine started in on me about backing Minnie Thomas for head of the school board. I mean, I always thought of Elaine as an *intelligent person* and then she starts this. She's probably glad I'm leaving."

Oh come on, Dottie, what's a little political disagreement among friends? The Minnie Thomases come and go, but a seven-year friendship is not to be tossed aside so quickly.

TELL EVERYBODY RIGHT AWAY!

When you're leaving a community, its absolutely essential to go through a period of mourning, yes, mourning, for the life you have led there, for the friendships you've formed.

Tell everybody the news right away and tell them how sad it makes you. (As for any fear of rejection, we explained to Dottie James, if so-called friends are really glad to see you go, you'll get the message right away. *Then* is the time to lay it on about the good life in the new location, not before the fact.)

Don't be shy about sentiment. If you feel like sitting down and having a good cry with your spouse or your best friend, by all means do so.

If this isn't your style, do something special to mourn your loss. Not just an ordinary party, but a get-together that brings back memories. It could be a farewell visit to a favorite restaurant with you picking up the check. It could be a dinner (or several dinners) at which you're careful to serve Ed's or Frances' favorite dish—the one he or she raved about, the time you cooked it in 1977. It could be a buffet of everyone's favorites, with home movies of good times past. It could be a sing along—insist that Carol bring her guitar and warn Phil he's going to be called on to play the piano, the way he did at the company Christmas party. It could be a last beach party or the all-night poker game to end all-night poker games. It could be anything your imagination dictates as long as it relates to the past, not the future. Have speeches and toasts to the old gang. Take plenty of pictures and pass them around.

This kind of celebration almost always ends up with expressions of sentiment that the participants didn't feel capable of, and often a certain amount of tears. Which is fine. That's what it's all about.

Loving farewells and nostalgic last get-togethers mean more than just assuring friends you are genuinely sorry to leave them. On a deeper level, they're essential to your emotional well-being. For what you are doing is going through the ritual of separation mourning—not for a death, to be sure, but for a part of your life that has ended.

THE IMPORTANCE OF MOURNING

When someone dies, we naturally mourn that person. Every culture since the beginning of recorded history has had its mourning ritual, though many did not understand why. Sigmund Freud was first to explain it scientifically. Mourning is a form of emotional catharsis, and, Freud said, failure to mourn can (and often does) result in one degree or another of pathological depression.

The normal mourning process includes a period of private grieving, time for venting grief through tears and talking it out with a trusted friend or counselor. The funeral ceremony, whatever form it takes, not only commemorates the dead person, but also invites the bereaved to accept the fact of death. Simultaneously, through the presence of friends, it offers reassurance that life will go on.

The entire chain is designed—or, more accurately, has evolved through folk wisdom—to help the bereaved adjust to life without the physical presence of the dead person, enriched by their memories of that person, but free to form new attachments.

What happens to those who deny the mourning process? And there are people who do, who refuse to discuss the dead person, refuse to attend the funeral, will not—or cannot—weep. Since they have not resolved their grief, they are left with feelings of emptiness, anxiety and depression that won't go away and can eventually manifest themselves in excessive drinking or pill dependency, psychosomatic ailments and various kinds of odd behavior.

You don't have to look for these people in medical journals. You hear about them or know them in real life. "He drinks, because he's never gotten over his wife's death." "She hasn't left the house since her mother died." "Of course she's hooked on pills, but then, her kid was killed in a car accident two years ago, and she hasn't been the same since."

To avoid social life or to seek the temporary relief of sedatives, tranquilizers or alcohol is not recommended though it is not abnormal behavior for one who has suffered a severe loss. The key word is *temporary*. Mourning a death is difficult at best. A few days or weeks of relying on crutches is not pathological.

But when the bereaved settle down into a psychological wheelchair, sometimes for life, the problem is not the death. It's usually the inability to mourn it properly.

WHO'S DEAD ANYWAY?

What, you may ask, has this to do with relocation? After all, nobody's dead.

No, nobody is, but a very particular past way of life *is* dead. The kinds of relationships you had with friends when you lived among them are no longer possible. Physical closeness is no longer possible. These are things that need to be mourned.

People who choose not to mourn, people who try to obliterate all memories of a way of life and the people involved in that way of life, run a similar risk to those who cannot mourn a death.

Running out, sneaking out or otherwise pretending that you don't care about leaving a community is, psychologically, the same as avoiding a funeral (because you hate funerals), or pretending to yourself that Marian, Herbert or Mother never died or that you don't really miss them.

We don't want to exaggerate. On leaving a community it's hardly necessary to mourn *everybody*. If you never could stand your neighbors Teddi and Stan, there's no need to put on crying scenes with them. Simply invite them to the public ceremonies (parties), much as you would distant cousins of the deceased.

But do go through the mourning ritual with those who have been closest. What you're accomplishing is accepting the fact, just as a bereaved person is, that you will no longer have day to day contact with these people. And you're incorporating, just as the bereaved person is, all the values you cherish in these people, even though they will be separated from you.

What you're taking within you (and along with you) is not merely a memory of a person lost forever, but memories or people you can still see three or four times a year; with whom you can communicate; with whom you can keep up a different but just as warm a relationship for the rest of your life.

At the same time, when you redefine your relationships with old friends you free yourself to make new friends in your new location, much as a fully realized period of mourning frees a widow or widower to find a new mate.

Make a special point of planning to write and of inviting old friends to come and visit in your new location. Sometimes the correspondence will dwindle away to yearly, newsy Christmas cards; with others it will flourish and deepen the ties of friendship.

Reiterate invitations to special friends and plan to visit them in return. If you can slowly build a circle of good friends that you can visit in various parts of the country, you're reaping one of the happiest rewards of the mobile life.

Note: we have talked of keeping up with friends, but keeping up with family is even more important, especially for children, who should know their grandparents, aunts and uncles. Do visit back and forth as much as is feasible. If you have a far-flung family, consider starting a cousins club. Or plan, if not once a year, at least once every few years, a full scale family reunion. Take this opportunity to think about how you will say good-bye to the people who are important to you. Try the following Leaving Exercise. Use it as a way to think about your good-byes and a way of ensuring that you'll feel good about them.

LEAVING EXERCISE

Write down the names of three (3) people you're going to miss.

	1)________	2)________	3)________
Their reaction when you say good-bye	1)	2)	3)
Your reaction when you say good-bye	1)	2)	3)
How would you like the interaction to be different?	1)	2)	3)

CHAPTER

9

PERSONAL REINVESTMENT: THE REAL SECRET OF SUCCESSFUL RELOCATION

No, right now we're not talking about selling your old house at a good price and putting your money into a new one without taking a loss (there's solid information on this in chapter 12). Here we're talking about the reinvestment of your emotional capital—your time, your interests, your commitment, your loyalty, in short—getting involved, *really involved,* in each new community and neighborhood you move to, even though you know you won't be there forever.

This investment has nothing to do with money. And yet it's best explained in the parlance of a financial transaction.

When you're born and grow up in a given community you hold an equity in that community by right of birth. You may be a *somebody* from the house on the hill, a *nobody* from the wrong side of the tracks or you may be from somewhere in between. But don't get us wrong; caste, class or economic pecking order aren't the point. *Belonging* is the point!

Non-movers, for the most part, can build on the foundation of their inherited emotional capital or they can diminish it by mismanagement. But the person who is born, lives and dies in a stable community usually inherits (and then expands) a supportive network of friends and relatives, a strong sense of personal identity and the reasonable expectation of a good turnout at the funeral.

It's very different for the movers, and this is where the financial analogy ceases. You can't transfer emotional capital like a bank account. Most of the young uprooted (the students, the newlyweds, the first jobbers) leave home with their emotional capital intact and are happy to reinvest it in the new community. They feel there's little or no risk entailed in making friends and commitments. Besides, they often reason, they're F.I.C.A. insured; if all is lost, they *can* go home again. The older movers—the suddenly transferred or suddenly fired in middle age—have the toughest relocation problem. It's understandable that they often resist reinvestment; the man who lost a fortune in the stock market may well want to keep his money in the mattress.

YOU'VE GOT TO GET INVOLVED

The process of getting really involved in a new community is the key to successful relocation.

Much of the literature and media coverage on relocation portrays it as a *necessarily* destructive psychological experience. Our experience has shown that this is not true.

It is the individuals and families who give up or for reasons they often don't understand can't reinvest who truly suffer. Those who remain committed to striving to make each new community a *home* avoid the effects.

"But how can I make a community home in two years?" many people ask. The answer is simple; it's like the myth of

Sisyphus. It's not reaching the top of the mountain that's most important but the benefits *derived from trying.*

A person's or family's *involvement* in a community reflects their identity, beliefs, attitudes, and values. One cannot give up the expression of his identity or values without suffering.

Some families and individuals find that reinvestment comes easily and naturally. Almost instinctively, they set about making themselves at home wherever they settle.

A fortunate few may go on relocating and reinvesting happily, and reaping the emotional benefits with compound interest for a lifetime. But these are the exceptions.

Since relocation is a continuing process, most transferees have a setback at one point or another (it happened to one couple we know after *seventeen* moves) when it simply becomes too much trouble to make the effort one more time.

But, if you do have such a setback, don't give up on reinvesting. It's a little like falling off a horse—if you don't get right back on, you may never get on again.

WATCH OUT FOR THE THIRD MOVE

The reinvestment problem usually surfaces at about the time of the third move. Lucy Ross's story is typical.

"The first move was exciting. I got married right out of college, and two months later Tim was transferred to St. Louis. Let me tell you, living in the big city after growing up in a dumb little town in the Midwest was exciting beyond my wildest dreams.

"We had no children then, so we went out a lot—the theater, movies, exploring the city. We made a lot of friends, mostly through the company, sometimes through my old college friends, and we partied a lot together. It was really like still being in school.

"Then we had Tim, Jr., and just as I was beginning to

realize that the apartment was too small, and the life we were leading didn't work anymore, Tim got transferred again, this time to Cleveland. Well, we bought a house in a suburb, Centre, a little house with a big mortgage. Just right for a couple with 1½ children.

"The Cleveland years I spent being a full-time mother. If you're a mother you meet a lot of other mothers. Tim was also making friends on his job. We still had, and went to, Saturday night parties (some couples brought their kids), and it was wine and cheese all the way. We really made a lot of good friends.

"At that point, Tim was transferred to Chicago. This was really a blow. I cried for days. When we got to Chicago, I just couldn't take an interest in the house, or meeting people, or anything. I missed my old friends so.

"Oh, I tried. We both tried. We went to Newcomers Club, we joined a church, I volunteered at the hospital—but life just wasn't fun anymore.

"Also, it's beginning to affect our marriage. I find myself snapping at Tim and the kids. After all, he has his job, but what have I got? On the other hand, I can't criticize him. I knew when we got married that we'd be moving around like this. Sure, eventually we'll be transferred out of Chicago, but I know already that it'll be more of the same, if not worse.

"We've talked it over and over, and find ourselves just talking in circles. We're just caught in a bind, and I don't see any way out."

HOW TO FACE THE TURNING POINT

It's hard not to sympathize with this all too familiar story. Lucy and Tim are indeed caught in a bind and, as Lucy correctly observed, it's nobody's fault. She and Tim are well ahead of the game in this respect; at this stage many wives accuse their husbands of putting the job first and neglecting wifely needs, and many husbands retaliate by accusing their wives of being lazy, self-centered, incompetent, or all three. The men rationalize, "If I can work my tail off to support this family, I don't see why *you* can't find some way to amuse yourself! Go take backgammon lessons or tennis lessons or join a bridge club, the way other women do."

Would that it were all that simple! If it were, there would be no need for this book.

Yes, there's a way out of the bind, and for the Lucys and Tims of this world, who have reached the turning point, the time to act is now.

First, they must carefully reevaluate Tim's career and their lifestyle in terms of *now*, not ten years ago:

1. Are his career goals the same?
2. Is he on his way to reaching them?
3. Does the job still hold the same satisfactions that it once gave?

If the answers are no and the emotional stress of moving is getting to be too much for both of them, perhaps it's time to get out of the game. There's no point in pumping a treadmill round and round with no worthwhile goal in sight. When that happens, the game has become, in a phrase made famous in the 1950s, a rat race.

TWO WHO STOPPED THE MUSIC

Nick and Jan Auster chose to get out of the rat race. In the early years of their marriage, Nick's company moved them six times. The last two moves were lateral. They made some friends along the way, but not many. But along the way they developed a great affinity for St. Louis. It was close to the town where Jan grew up, and she was happy there. When the company gave Nick his marching orders one more time, Jan was as sick at heart about the move as Lucy was about leaving Cleveland.

They thought the impending move through together—all the way through. Nick realized that he had reached a plateau in his career. He was a technical man, a computer systems analyst, and realized that promotion to line executive was not for him. Indeed, he didn't even want it. His future with the company was clearly charted: a series of moves from one installation to another, with perhaps small raises every time, and the security of the pension plan. Besides, neither he nor Jan enjoyed the excitement of living in new places and finding new people. They figured out that they were stay-at-homes at heart, and that it only made sense to act accordingly.

So Nick turned down the transfer. Instead, he found a good job with the city, complete with pension plan, benefits, and modest raises, in which he could use his skills. Now the whole family could enjoy the community they had come to call home.

What Nick and Jan did was get out of the reinvestment market. They put their emotional capital into low yield, but no risk savings plans. It worked for them, which meant that it was right for them.

TWO WHO TRIED AGAIN

Tom and Lucy were different. On our advice, they tried the same reevaluation plan. Unlike Nick, Tom still derived enormous satisfaction from his job and the future looked bright. Lucy took the high risk/low risk moving test and found herself to be, much to her surprise, a very low risk. In counseling sessions she came to realize that her problem was not that relocation was too difficult for her; it was (or had been, up to that point) entirely too easy!

Lucy is a gregarious, outgoing person. She makes friends wherever she goes. By her own testimony, she did so in New York. She did so in Cleveland. With no apparent effort, the friends came, or so she believed at the time, with the territory.

In Cleveland there were no old college friends, no more young mothers in the park (the kids were almost teen-agers now) and no crummy apartments or old houses to fix up. With Tom's new job came a three bedroom ranch in the suburbs.

Lucy learned that as life goes on, especially for mobile couples, circumstances change. Lucy's original position was that of the small investor who always made out without even trying; but when the first reverse takes place, panics. This investor takes the money and runs.

Lucy was ready, when we first saw her, to take all the emotional capital she had already invested (and the accrued interest) and throw it down the drain without even trying to reassess her chances. After a searching self-examination she realized that, even without college chums, or small children she had depended on in early life, she had a real talent for readjusting. She could do it one more (or a lot more) times. And so she did.

She joined the Newcomer's Club and suggested setting up a crafts group. She was, somewhat to her surprise, joined by other women with an interest in crafts. She continued to attend church but now, because she loves to sing, as she put it, "*got up my nerve* to try out for the choir."

Her nerve paid off. She reported back to us. "Our crafts group is planning a crafts fair in the spring! Who knows, I might start a crafts boutique. And, since the choir accepted me I'm taking lessons in sight reading."

That was three years ago. It would be nice to report that Lucy is the author of a best-selling needlepoint book or singing with the Metropolitan Opera. She isn't. She's something even better—an adult woman, happy with her life and with herself.

Tim was transferred last year to a western city. Recently we got a letter from Lucy. "Tim's new job is great, I'm teaching crafts at a school for retarded children (I even get *paid*), and even though I never did learn to sight read, I'm singing second soprano with the Sweet Adelines. It's just a bunch of women who like to sing harmony, but it's fun. And I've made so many good friends." Lucy has passed the turning point with flying colors. She's on her way.

Lucy's Secret

Lucy's newfound contentment in the mobile life has nothing to do with her ability to sing or do needlepoint. It has to do with her new willingness *to take risks.*

For Lucy, who was not accustomed to taking a leader role, to suggest the formation of the crafts group at Newcomers *was a risk.* She could have been politely turned down. But once she took this risk and succeeded, she found it much easier, in the next town, to apply for her school job. A little success can go a long way, if not now, then later.

Trying out for the choir was even more of a risk for her since she was painfully aware of her lack of formal training in music. But being accepted made it much easier for her to try out for the Sweet Adelines (who are not, by the way, just a bunch of women who like to sing harmony, but a nationally organized network of amateur women singers with many local chapters, and they're pretty particular about whom they take in).

RISK TAKING: THE GAME THAT PAYS OFF

Like any other form of investment, personal reinvestment requires that you take some risks.

In a new community, the first risk is social, fear of rejection. The people we'd like to make friends with might not want to make friends with us.

Jack Montgomery was a talented New York public relations

man. He was hired away, at a significant increase in salary, by a client firm, located in a small New England town. His wife, Marylou, who was used to being wined and dined on the company expense account and enjoyed the atmosphere of bonhommie that generally prevails in the public relations business, was thrilled about the move. It meant a beautiful new house, the extra money they'd been searching for to put the kids through college and generally a whole new life.

Six months after they made the move, Marylou was thoroughly disillusioned. "This company he works for is not to be *believed*," she said. "I mean, after all, Jack's a vice-president. But have any of those stuffy executives even invited us to dinner? No.

"Of course, I know what it's all about. They think we're just pushy New Yorkers. I mean okay, so we didn't come over on the Mayflower. That's no reason they can't be polite."

That's Marylou's version. We also heard the other side of the story from Esther Honeywell, a sweet, small-town New England lady, who is the wife of the president of Jack's company.

"You know," she said, "we've just hired the most remarkable young man, Mr. Montgomery. We got him away from Mitchell-Cameron, a really big New York public relations firm, and he's going to do just wonders for the company, I'm sure. Of course I'm a little intimidated by having these important New York people in our little family. I mean what am I supposed to do—invite them over for a New England boiled dinner?"

"By all means," we told her. "They'd love it." So would any displaced person who desperately wants to join in and be part of the local ways.

There's another side to this social coin; Esther and her husband would like very much to be invited to Jack and Marylou's house for whatever entertainment Jack and Marylou want to provide. (Esther confesses a weakness to try a real New York style cocktail party with fancy hors d'oeuvres.) For her part, Marylou would be thrilled by the hominess of a real New England clambake.

If you're new in a community, don't stand on ceremony. Yes, it is customary, by Emily Post rules, for the employer to invite the employee first. But Emily Post went out with World War II. Don't become hung up on social conventions, real or imaginary.

Our advice to Esther, invite Jack and Marylou to a real down home New England dinner. Our simultaneous advice to Marylou, invite Esther and H.J. to a New York style buffet party or a cookout.

This is called breaking down imagined social or business precedents, or good public relations or just plain making friends. It's also called—don't try ESP and attempt to divine what's in another person's head.

Of course some of the time it doesn't work. An Esther may turn down the invitation of a Marylou. A Marylou may invite an Esther to a party that turns out to be a complete fiasco. But this is the risk you take. The worst thing that can happen is that you don't make social friends with the boss or you waste an evening. However, on the percentages, taking the risk works most of the time.

HOW TO SAY HELLO

A question we're often asked in workshops is, "It's all very well to say join this, join that, go to parties, or lend out your lawnmower; but what do I *say* to people at parties and meetings to break the ice? How do I let my neighbor know he can borrow my lawnmower if I can't get up the nerve to say 'hello'? I'm a pretty reserved person."

You are not alone. Dale Carnegie made a fortune by recognizing this fact. It's fashionable to knock his simplistic approach, but most sophisticated therapists are aware that Mr.

Carnegie was on to something in *How To Win Friends and Influence People.*

The Carnegie method, psychological studies and the political know-how of your Uncle Matthew, three times Mayor of Backwater, Arkansas, concur on one point. Everybody likes to be liked, not just you, the other fellow, too. Once you know that, you're half way there.

HI, NEIGHBOR!

The first people you're likely to come in contact with in your new location are the people next door. They may not become your best friends, but you certainly want to get to know them. That first encounter may be crucial, as illustrated by the following dialogues.

In each scenario, the situation is the same. The transferee, setting out to get the morning paper, runs into the neighbor, who is going off to work.

Dialogue 1

TRANSFEREE: Hi!

NEIGHBOR: Hi!

TRANSFEREE: My name is Jim Santo. We just moved in next door.

NEIGHBOR: Glad to meet you.

TRANSFEREE: We got in last night, and we're feeling sort of disoriented. It's nice to see a friendly face.

NEIGHBOR: Yeah.

TRANSFEREE: We had kind of a rough time. We lived in Oklahoma for about seven years, and then the company decided to move us. We didn't want to go, but of course I had no choice. You never do. So here we are. I hope we're going to like it. I never lived in the East before.

NEIGHBOR: Well, it's not too bad. It can be rough at first, though.

TRANSFEREE: Oh, you bet. Moving, unpacking, all that stuff, not to mention the drive out, with the dog and all. I'm really beat.

NEIGHBOR: Moving is never easy.

TRANSFEREE: Well, this time was the worst.

NEIGHBOR: Yeah, well, good to meet you.

TRANSFEREE: Good to meet you. Hope to see you soon.

NEIGHBOR: Right. Have a good day.

TRANSFEREE: Bye.

NEIGHBOR: Bye.

Dialogue 2

TRANSFEREE: Hi, how are you?

NEIGHBOR: Pretty good.

TRANSFEREE: My name is Bill Alvarez and we just moved in.

NEIGHBOR: Good to meet you.

TRANSFEREE: What's your name?

NEIGHBOR: Ed McGhee.

TRANSFEREE: Well, nice to know you, Ed. You married?

NEIGHBOR: Oh sure. Two kids. My wife's name is Pat.

TRANSFEREE: Mine is Sherri. Were you good friends with the people who lived here before?

NEIGHBOR: Yeah. They were here about eight years and we were pretty close to them.

TRANSFEREE: Boy! That's rough. I know how you feel. We were very friendly with the couple next door where we came from and we sure hated to leave them. It's really tough being moved around.

NEIGHBOR: It sure is! I've moved myself, so I know.

TRANSFEREE: Hey, I don't want to impose on you, but we're going to need some help getting to know what goes on around here. I wonder if my wife could drop in and see your wife some time?

NEIGHBOR: Sure thing. Pat's been looking forward to meeting the new neighbors.

TRANSFEREE: That's super, really super. Maybe you and I can get together sometime too.

NEIGHBOR: I'd like to do that.

TRANSFEREE: Well, I don't want to keep you. I know you have to get to work. That's one break. I don't have to report for work for a week.

NEIGHBOR: Oh no? They gave you a week off, huh? Where are you going to be working?

TRANSFEREE: At the chemical plant downtown—so it's not a bad commute.

NEIGHBOR: Good. Say—are you two doing anything special tonight?

TRANSFEREE: No.

NEIGHBOR: Well, then, why don't you come by about 8:30, and bring Sherri with you. Then we can all get to know each other.

TRANSFEREE: That would be really great! Sherri will be real pleased.

NEIGHBOR: It's set then. Okay, Bill, nice to meet you and see you later.

In the first dialogue, the transferee, Jim, did not get to know his neighbor. In fact, he didn't even bother to ask his name. Instead, he started the conversation with complaints about leaving his former location and the difficulties of moving, all of which were of minimal interest to his new neighbor.

In the second, the transferee, Bill, engaged his new neighbor in conversation by asking him not only his name but how he felt about losing his former neighbors. This led to a discussion comparing experiences, and the conversation ended with the neighbor inviting the transferee and his wife over that evening.

A basic rule for starting up a conversation: try to find a common interest and then get the other person talking about it. Bear in mind the story about the congressman who spent almost a whole evening explaining his ideas about the international situation to his dinner partner and later labelled her, "the most fascinating conversationalist I've met in a long time."

MORE WAYS TO MEET NEIGHBORS

When you visit a store for the first time, introduce yourself to the storekeeper: "I'm Mrs. Carmody and we're new in the neighborhood. You certainly have a wonderful selection of fresh vegetables!"

On meeting a suburban neighbor with a child: "Hi, I'm Jenny Cantor—we just moved in up the block. What a pretty little girl!"

Or a city neighbor walking his dog: "Hi! I'm Al Burns, we just moved into the building. That's a nice looking Doberman you've got there!"

Commenting on a neighbor's child, dog, or car or garden is an almost surefire conversation starter. So is the specific question. It can be asked in two ways.

Wrong Way

"I just can't seem to find my way around this town! Maybe you could tell me something about the stores."

This is most likely to elicit the answer, "Be glad to. Someday when we both have time, I'll drive you around."

Right Way

"I need to get a prescription filled. Can you recommend a good drugstore?"

"Oh, yes. We always go to Mason's on the corner of Commerce and Main. They're awfully nice and they deliver. Have you found a good cleaner, yet? If not, try . . ."

People love to give advice—*if* they know specifically what advice is wanted.

PARTY ICE BREAKERS

At a social gathering where you know no one, walk up to someone who is seemingly disengaged and say, "Hi! How do you know Tom and Margot?"

The answer may be, "I went to school with Tom, I work with Margot. I'm their cousin" (or whatever).

Your response: "I went to school with Margot. I'm Tom's colleague [boss, secretary]."

It doesn't matter whether it's a conversation about work, school, or whatever. Most of the time the disengaged person is just as eager for conversational material as you are.

Or comment on some feature of the house or decor.

"Tom and Margot have a really well-planned kitchen. Do you like to cook?"

"I love those little antique chairs. Margot really has a feel for decorating."

Or, "That funny plant with the stripey leaves is pretty. Do you know what it's called?"

Cooking and decorating are of interest to some. But *everybody* (well almost everybody) has house plants.

THE PUBLIC MEETING

You get points for sitting in the audience, but you make personal connections during the coffee break. The same rules apply as to private parties—make overtures—but at public meetings, you have more to work with. Zero in on someone who is unoccupied at the coffee table. While filling your cup, engage him or her in conversation. Some openers: "The coffee is good here. I really needed it." And, if you get a smile, "This is certainly a lively meeting. Of course, I'm new in town and don't know what to think."

This gives your opposite number the opportunity to discuss coffee or, more important, what he or she thinks about the opinions advanced at the meeting. If the stranger happens to be a newcomer like yourself, right away you have an ally.

SOME DON'TS

Don't start a conversation at a gathering of any kind by criticizing the host or hostess, criticizing their home, criticizing the food or drink at a party. ("Oh dear. They don't have any white wine.") Or criticizing the new town. Or criticizing *anything*. Stay neutral and keep smiling.

This goes double for public meetings. Resist saying to a brand new acquaintance, "That's really the most *boring* speech on women's rights I've *ever* heard," or, "Can you believe that *idiot* councilman?"

Bear in mind that the feminist speaker *may* be your new friend's cousin, the councilman, his uncle.

We advocate initiating conversations, but *not* by strong-arm methods.

OF COURSE, YOU CAN OVERDO IT

"Hi. I'm Kathy Jenson and I've been dying to meet you. I've heard all about the fascinating job you have with the Human Resources Commission—you're pretty famous in this town, you know. And I want to hear all about it. I'd like to get into politics myself someday. Come on, let's sit down over there and talk about it. . . ."

"So you're the famous Ted Arthur! Believe me, I heard a lot about you before we got here and I think there are some deals we could work out. It's pretty noisy in here. Come on, let's go into the next room and talk."

Or if it's a group engaged in conversation: "Hi! Mind if I join you? I'm Lou Baker and I'm new in town. I heard you talking about your problem with the water supply, and I think there are some pointers I can give you on how to solve it. Now in the last place I lived . . ."

Make the first move when you meet new people. But let them make the second. Don't try to take over all at once.

BEWARE OF BAD MOUTHERS

In any community there's somebody who doesn't like something.

Beware of the new acquaintance who tells you right away, "Don't get involved with Mary Smith. She's a troublemaker. Nobody can stand her."

Or, "Stay away from Fred Sands. He's bad news."

Reserve judgment on any individual until you've met that individual. Keep in mind that the person most anxious to tell you everyone's faults is usually bad news himself. You may find Mary or Fred good company.

Keep an open mind. It's better to make good friends slowly than the wrong friends too quickly.

Don't take sides until you've heard all of them.

HOW TO HANDLE CLIQUES

A problem we hear about frequently, especially from women transferees, is cliques. Sometimes the problem is real. Priscilla Johnson, a New Englander transplanted to a small Texas city, tried her best to get involved in charitable and volunteer activities, but was ever so politely cold-shouldered.

Finally, a friendly neighbor explained it to her. "Look, honey," she said. "You're just wasting your time. A lot of the women in this town don't think anybody's *anybody* unless she qualifies for the Daughters of the Alamo. And I should know, because I *am* one. So you're not going to get anywhere with those charity ladies."

Priscilla was shocked, hurt and just plain outraged by this news. Her neighbor laughed. "Now don't get on your Yankee high horse," she said. "I suppose it's wrong, but that's the way it *is* in this town."

"Tell you what," she said, "some of us are starting a chapter of the League of Women Voters—shake things up a little, if you know what I mean. And you'd just fit in fine." And indeed Priscilla did.

Sometimes the cliques are strictly in the imagination of the beholder. Nellie Munn, an accountant with a chemical company, was, at age thirty-nine, transferred to a California city.

An attractive divorcee, she was sure the California life was for her. She moved into a condominium complex with a swimming pool and social center. Many of the residents were single like herself. Contrary to her expectations, she hated it.

"I go to the pool every evening," she said, "and what do I find? A bunch of swinging singles aged twenty-five, running around and pushing each other into the water; some young marrieds who stick together and talk about their children; some old people who sit together and talk about retirement plans.

"In my age group, there are a lot of interesting looking

people, but they're so *cliquey*. They all sit together up at the north end of the pool and only talk to each other. I've watched them; they even have their beach chairs staked out. None of them has ever said so much as hello to me."

"Why not," we asked Nellie, "try saying hello to *them*? Or just sitting near them?"

Nellie took our advice, naive as it sounded. One sunny Sunday, instead of isolating herself with her suntan lotion and library novel, she plunked herself down right in the middle of the clique, asking brightly if the seat were taken.

Indeed it wasn't. Nor, apporently, was the attractive looking man in the next chair, who said, "My name is Frank. What's yours? *We've been wondering who you were.*"

Well, Nellie told Frank who she was, and Frank told Nellie who he was, and the upshot of it all was that Nellie got introduced all around and eventually was asked if she'd like to join the Board of Managers of the condominium. They needed an accountant badly.

HOW TO REINVEST: STEP BY STEP

When you settle into a new community, your first tactical steps will obviously be the practical moves toward the necessities. Check out local stores and services. Find out where the supermarket is, the nearest drugstore, the best dry cleaners, the cheapest gas station, the best bank for your particular needs.

Connecting up with relatively hassle free suppliers of these essentials takes first priority.

In a really small town, you can generally survey and evaluate the shopping and services scene with a quick drive around the downtown area or the nearest shopping center. In bigger cities, you"ll need help.

Simply asking a neighbor is a very good way of seeking and finding help. And it has a built-in plus value. Asking the woman next door about where to find the best food bargains and the best priced gas is also a great way to meet the family next door. An ancient rule that's always worth remembering: most people love being asked for advice; it makes them feel knowledgeable and important. Which they are, especially to you at this stage of your mobile life.

Of course the neighbor may prove unnecessary. You may be met on your doorstep by a Welcome Wagon representative even before the china is uncrated. Welcome Wagon people are in business to promote local business and they make no secret of that. But they're also full of information about their client banks, supermarkets, dress shops and whatever you'll be needing.

Do welcome Welcome Wagon. You may not be interested in buying most products of their clients at the moment. But who knows about the future? Meanwhile the local Welcome Wagon lady (or gentleman) is also well informed about shopping, who's who and what's what in the area, and will be glad to share this information with an inquisitive, genuinely interested newcomer.

HERE ARE THE PRIORITIES

You'll be busy uncrating the china, unpacking the books, putting them on the shelves, arranging the furniture, attending to necessary repairs around the house. Nobody needs to be reminded that this is a *lot of work*. Hard work. Suggestion— do it now. Later you'll be glad you did. Look at it this way; the sooner you make your house livable, the sooner you can begin living.

If you have a child or children, getting started on the process of getting him or her or them enrolled in school is a natural top priority too.

If all this keeps you busy (if not frantic) for at least a week, remember, on the seventh day, you're allowed to rest.

This is the day to take the kids for a walk in the park, to see the local wonders, dine on pushcart food or at the best (1) seafood, 2) chili or pastrami, or (3) truck drivers' diner in the vicinity.

Next week, it's back to business. Even if you haven't yet found the ideal supermarket, gotten the curtains up in the living room, or established yourself with a bank, you have the satisfaction of knowing that you've *started* on some projects.

So start some new ones. Look around for groups to join: a church or synagogue, a service organization or other formal organizations in which you can become involved.

At the same time, find yourself a doctor and a dentist. This is a problem that baffles many movers. There are several answers. A local medical center that provides all services for a set fee is a good one for the family not covered or not completely covered by medical insurance. If nothing else avails, call the county medical society. But the best way usually is to ask a doctor or dentist you trusted in your former location to recommend someone in the new place. If he doesn't know anyone to recommend, he probably knows somebody at a hospital in your new city, who can recommend local talent.

After that, comes the business of making friends, and there are ever so many, many ways of going about this treasure hunt.

MAKING FRIENDS: HERE'S HOW

The A-1 top priority rule for meeting new people is—don't wait for them to approach you, approach them! There are all kinds of formal channels to try. Many communities have meetings of newcomers clubs designed to make newcomers welcome. Go. You may love it. Many newcomers groups have sub-groups that specialize in every activity you can think of from bowling to backgammon. You may also hate it. If you do, our earnest advise is not to give up on finding some birds of your own feather.

When Barbara Carroll moved to a small New Jersey community and attended a newcomers club meeting she was appalled and downright embarrassed, "All they did was sing college songs," she said. "I don't know any college songs. Besides, I'm tone deaf."

She didn't grin and bear it. She found another channel. She's a natural foods enthusiast and soon discovered in her neighborhood a co-op grocery store that specialized in organically grown foodstuffs. She volunteered to help out and found not only a number of like-minded friends, but an unpaid job as public relations director for the store. (She just placed her first story in the local paper.)

A 100 percent guaranteed way to meet people is to join them: churches, synagogues, women's clubs, men's service organizations. Better yet, special interest groups: friends of the environment, little theater groups, Little League, you name it. If you don't know whether such groups exist, the women's editor of the local paper can help you. And don't neglect branches of your alumni organization, sorority and fraternity connections or chapters of any organization you have belonged to in another community.

How to Volunteer

Another way is volunteering, but proceed with caution and without excessive expectations. In many communities, volunteer groups are not only service but social organizations. Don't barge in and expect to be made a member of the hospital committee right away just because you had made the grade in your old hometown. You're new here, remember? The important jobs in any volunteer organization, just as in a business organization, are awarded on a basis of seniority or distinguished service or local connections (business, family, etc). Be prepared to start small.

The same goes for political groups with one further warning: stick to presidential (or senatorial or gubernatorial) campaigns, at least until you've surveyed the local scene for a while. In small-town politics (and often in big city politics, too!) things are not always as they seem. Party labels can be misleading or meaningless. Plunging into a local political fight when you're not familiar with the personalities and underlying issues may mark you as an obnoxious newcomer; or make you more enemies than friends; or put you in bed with the wrong bedfellows.

Taking courses can bring you into contact with like-minded people (and besides that, possibly further the training of a newly career-minded wife or newly advancement-minded husband). If you can teach courses, this offers many advantages, too. If you have a special area of expertise, offer it. If you can teach communications skills, economics or business English in adult night school at a nearby university, by all means offer to do so. You may be surprised to find yourself regarded not as a poorly paid teacher (and you *will* be poorly paid), but as a welcome visiting expert. If you enjoy working with children, athletic teams need coaches, Boy Scouts and Girl Scouts need leaders—and you meet a lot of parents that way.

The Neighborhood Connection

Making connections through groups and community activities is almost invariably worthwhile and productive. Establishing yourself as a good neighbor on the street where you live is equally worthwhile and possibly even more important. No matter what gadding about you may choose to pursue, your neighborhood is after all, home. Your neighbors are the people you live among, the people you see every day and quite possibly (since, if you've been following the rules, you have selected them to live among) your most likely future friends or at least acquaintances. And if you don't care for the people next door or across the street, there's always a selection of more folks up and down the street or on the next block or two or three.

When you move into a neighborhood, don't wait for the people up the street to pay you a call. Very few people do this any more. If you're good at entertaining, begin by holding an open house or backyard barbecue for your new neighbors. Will they think this presumptuous? Ninety percent of the time, no! But if some do, forget them! You and your family may see yourselves as unsure newcomers, and most people coming will empathize with that and be supportive. Go easy on impression making; tune in on the routine atmosphere of your neighborhood. Your cue, if you're indeed city folk, is to entertain *simply*. Never mind the smoked whitefish. Serve the hot dogs and hamburgers, fresh salads and good conversation. Provide plenty of soft drinks, beer, and, for those who feel the need, a supply of the hard stuff. If you (the wife) have a special pecan pie, bake it. If you (the husband) are an expert in grilling chicken, do so.

Putting Your Best Head Forward

Let's turn it around. You're not sophisticated city folk. You are (according to your own view of yourselves) a country couple suddenly plunged into an economically intimidating milieu. Surprising as it may seem, the rules are exactly the same. Invite your new neighbors to a housewarming. Do your own thing, whatever it is. Hamburgers, hot dogs, special pecan pie, special grilled chicken, good conversation. While less sophisticated neighbors may be intimidated or turned off by conspicuous efforts to impress, up-scale neighbors will be bored.

How to win friends in a new neighborhood boils down to a simple maxim: *be your own best selves.* If new acquaintances are unresponsive or unappreciative, you can do without them as friends.

Once you've met everyone, don't be shy about offering practical evidence of friendship in terms of goods and services. The woman who is willing not only to lend her punchbowl to the day care center for their open house, but bake cookies for the local Girl Scout drive is labeled a good scout herself. The teen-ager who proclaims her (or his) availability for baby sitting (or helping out at parties) is a neighborhood asset. The man who is not only willing to lend his power mower but happens to be an expert at opening accidentally locked car doors with a wire coat hanger may find himself an overnight social success.

Loving thy neighbor helps, but it's not enough. Helping thy neighbor integrates you into your new-home extended family—your neighborhood.

Do keep remembering: the more you put into a community, the more you get out of it.

Remember, too, that people differ and that you're hardly under the gun. There is no set timetable. Don't panic if you're going slowly or are having some ups and downs. This is normal; reinvestment is not a steady upward climb. People often go through periods of feeling discouraged and lonely before going on to a perfectly good adjustment.

REINVESTMENT PROGRESS REPORT

This questionnaire will help you keep track of how you are progressing towards emotional reinvestment in your new community.

The twelve objectives listed are those that help most people feel at home in a new place. They're explained on the next page.

Every two weeks after arrival, rate yourself on whether you are achieving or adequately pursuing each objective. For each *no*, try to evaluate why you're not making progress and what you can do differently to improve the situation.

Eight to nine *yes* answers after twelve weeks means you are well on your way to successful reinvestment.

Reinvestment Objectives

1. Friendships. This consists of finding people who are potential close relationships.
2. Support Systems and Security Relationships. These are the people and groups that can be supportive in an emotional way, i.e., church, synagogue, newcomers club, etc. Also, those relationships which lend a feeling of predictability and safety in a situation, i.e., doctors, dentists, gas station, a neighbor that could be called upon for help.
3. Commitment to new home. This category consists of getting to the tasks that need to be accomplished and give you a sense you've invested yourself in your home, i.e., painting, landscaping, furniture buying, etc.
4. Play Activities. Seeking out the resources in community to satisfy recreational needs, i.e., tennis, bowling, movies, bridge clubs, etc.
5. Settling into daily routine. Here you should assess if if you have a daily routine, how comfortable it is, are you becoming progressively more relaxed with this routine.
6. Organizations. In this category you should rate whether you are pursuing getting involved in whatever groups seem meaningful to you.
7. Establish store preferences. You should rate the progress you are making toward establishing preferred places to shop, getting known in some of them and feeling comfortable there.

8. Mutually supportive family behavior. This consists of evaluating whether the family is pulling together to resolve the issues of moving for each member.
9. Establishing new ties for children. Consider if your children are making friends, joining groups, etc., and if not are you helping this effort.
10. Parent establishing relationship with school. If you have children, rate your feeling of getting known by and knowing pepole at the school so communications about your children can be set up.
11. Maintain old ties. Rate whether or not you are maintaining contact with those you and your family had close relationships with in previous community.
12. Job adjustment. Assess how comfortable you are feeling with your co-workers, daily routine and work. Are you satisfied with your job performance?

Please turn the page for the Community Reinvestment Progress Report.

COMMUNITY REINVESTMENT PROGRESS REPORT

Reinvestment Objectives	2 wks		4 wks		6 wks		8 wks		12 wks	
	Yes	No	Yes	No	Yes	No	Yes	No	Yes	No
1. Friendships										
2. Support systems and security relationships										
3. Commitment to new home										
4. Play activities										
5. Settling daily routine										
6. Organizations										
7. Establish store preferences										
8. Mutually supportive family behavior										
9. Establishing new ties for children										
10. Parent establishing relationship with school										
11. Maintain old ties										
12. Job adjustment										

"BUT WHAT ABOUT MY JOB?"

Twenty years ago, this question, coming from a woman, would have been rhetorical, if asked at all.

The wife of William H. Whyte's *Organization Man* (the best seller about corporate life in the 1950s) didn't have a job. If she worked at all outside the home, it was usually on a part-time or marginal basis, reading to children's groups, helping a divorced friend start a dress shop, serving for pin money as a "stringer" writing at space rates for a weekly newspaper.

When her husband was transferred, she had few qualms about giving up her job because she usually equated it in her own mind with a hobby, except that she sometimes got paid for it. There would be other dress shops, other weeklies, other volunteer activities. Besides, her real job was being wife, mother, hostess and backstop for her husband. Where he went, she went.

Times have changed, as everybody knows, and more and more people are beginning to accept, even men, that today most women, including wives, work. The woman who is totally supported by her husband is the exception, not the rule. The Bureau of Labor Statistics defines a typical American family, for the purpose of trend analysis, as consisting of mom, dad and two kids living at home. In this family 93 percent of the time mom has a job—and often it's not just a job but a career. Outside the "typical" family a number of sources have estimated that 51.9 percent of spouses work.

When the organization man of the 1950s had to pack up and move, his main considerations were what the move meant to his job, his family's lifestyle and the children's schooling.

His 1980s counterpart must often deal with one more factor added to the mix—the organization woman with whom he shares his life.

She may make less money than he does, though not necessarily. Her job may be less important, she may *care* even more about her life outside the home than her husband does. He never had to fight for his independence from the vacuum cleaner.

NO MORE RING AROUND THE COLLAR!

"It took me seven years to work up from secretary to sales representative for my company," Helen Kramer told us angrily. "I was the first woman in that male chauvinist pig outfit to break out of the secretary typecasting and I'm damned if I'm going back to playing ring around the collar just because Herb's company is sending Herb to Chicago."

"Sure I want to move up to Kansas City," said Hank Tolliver. "But what about Nora? Now that the kids are teenagers, she's just getting started on the career she always wanted. She's got her M.A. and she's an instructor at the state university. She doesn't make a lot of mony, but she's on her way."

Hank is management. But his blue collar co-worker, Mike Mason, has the same problem. His wife Sally doesn't have a career—she has a job, and it's a good one. As a billing machine operator in a unionized shop, she makes more money than Nora will for some years and almost as much as her husband. The Masons count on Sally's income. A number of authorities indicate that the Mason's reliance on Sally's income will become the rule rather than the exception in the economy of the eighties.

And now Mike is being transferred in a big group move. All his friends are going. "How can I go?" Mike asked us. "There's no job for Sally in Martindale. At least not like this one. She makes top scale, has seniority and there's plenty of overtime. Between us, Sally and I make $30,000 a year. Without her income—well, forget college for the kids!"

To complicate matters still further, today 5–10 percent of transferred workers *are* women. It may be Helen Kramer, not Herb, who gets sent to Chicago. Sally Mason, not Mike, whose division is moved.

And in the near future, it will be Nora, too.

The present-day Nora, married in the fifties, put off the graduate work that would qualify her as a professional woman and took time out to have babies. Her younger counterparts tend to reverse the order. College women today don't put first priority on marriage after graduation, as did most of their mothers and practically all their grandparents. Most young women include marriage and children as part of their life plan, but they give their own careers equal (sometimes more) importance. In 1970 less than 5 percent of those enrolled in business and professional graduate schools were female. Today the figure approaches 50 percent. These women are obviously serious—very serious—about their careers.

"Which means" so the *Wall Street Journal* predicts, "five to ten years from now, when these women and the men they marry come up for promotion, companies will be four to ten times as likely to see [relocation] problems." There will be far more problems for the couples, too. Several recent studies of corporate couples refusing transfer indicate that between 25–33 percent list dual-career concerns as the primary reason.

HIS, HERS, THEIRS

Future projections aside: at present, in the overwhelming majority of white-collar families, there's one career (his) and one job (hers).

All other things being equal, if he's transferred, she gives up her job and goes along. If she's asked to relocate, her almost automatic answer is "Sorry. I'm married." Everybody understands.

It makes economic good sense (although this is no longer always the case). In the changing roles of the sexes, which we hear so much about, the reality lags somewhat behind the dream. In most families, he's still the major breadwinner; he still has the greater opportunity for raises and promotions; and when push comes to shove, it's his career, not her job, that's usually providing medical benefits for the family, retirement benefits for the couple and money to put the kids through school. Her job is supplementary income—helpful but not essential.

Except, probably, to her.

A year ago, we met Frank and Fran Ferris. Frank, an assistant personnel manager for his company, was being relocated from the northeast to the southwest. Fran, a well paid secretary to an insurance company, had no qualms at all about going along. "What's to worry?" she said. "I'm a good secretary and I can get a job anywhere. I type ninety words a minute."

Mark Manning, a salesman, was also part of the group. And his wife Martha was also a secretary. She worked in the administrative office of a small college. She also could type. She was not very well paid, but to make up for this her job entitled her to tuition-free courses.

Martha agreed to move, but a month before the move was to take place Mark woke up to find his wife sitting by the window of their bedroom and crying.

"It was all about her *job*," Mark told us. "She said she would miss her *job*! Now I ask you, what kind of a job is it that pays you $4,000 a year? Oh sure, she gets summers off, has a lot of fun hanging around with students and professors and taking courses. She's with her own kind. She's got a B.A., which is more than I have. She's attractive, good on the phone and types ninety words a minute. I could get her a job with my own company as an executive secretary that would pay three times what she's getting now. She's just not ambitious enough."

Martha told a different story.

"I can imagine what Mark said," she said. "She has a B.A., I don't! I've heard that till I'm blue in the face. He's the big success, I'm the little wife.

"Well, that's the way I wanted it too, when we got married. But that was fifteen years ago. Mark was the most exciting man I ever me. All the boys I went to school with were being hippies or dropouts and Mark already had a good job with a big company. His father worked in the shop with that company—did you know that?

"I could never hope to equal his success," she continued, "but I did want to do something on my own. I know I could make more money as a secretary—but the reason I'm working at the college is that I'm going for my M.A. I want to be a teacher, not a typist. But how can I tell him that?"

"Just the way you told it to us," we said. And Martha did. Not at all surprisingly, it worked.

An Extreme Case

Martha and Mark were a case of extreme Rashomonitis—lack of communication between those who should, through mutual love, communicate best.

What Martha didn't realize:

1. That much as he acknowledged her skills, her B.A. was a great source of pride to Mark, the self-made man.
2. That he wanted her to be ambitious—but didn't understand what forms her ambition took.

What Mark didn't realize:

1. That Martha was not a natural born go-getter, as he was.
2. That a college degree, B.A. or M.A., is only a certificate of progress and union card to a profession, not a mark of social prestige.
3. That Martha had grown close to her colleagues and would miss them.

What both didn't realize, they loved each other enough to work it all out.

Which they did.

Mark and Martha are now settled comfortably in the new location. Recently we got a letter from Martha.

"Everything is working out fine. I'm taking courses at the State University and at the end of the year will have my M.A. Keep your fingers crossed. I'm also *making money* transcribing tapes at home for the sales promotion department. Would you believe: $45 a tape!

"Of course, Mark still isn't satisfied. Wouldn't you know? Now he wants me to go for a Ph.D., and when I asked why, he said 'So I can brag about my wife, the doctor!' That man: He may just talk me into it."

He may or may not, which is not important. What's important is that his career and her career are now in equilibrium to the satisfaction of both. He has his, she has hers, and they have theirs—a newly strengthened marriage.

Mark and Martha were able to work out their problem because they were willing and able to be honest with each other. And because each was aware of (and cared about) the other's needs.

Unfortunately it doesn't always work that way.

WINNERS AND LOSERS

Chet Shroeder was a product manager for a New York based company. His wife Marcia was a buyer for a New York store. Chet approved thoroughly of Marcia's job. Not only did she bring home a substantial pay check; she was the best dressed wife in the division, and Chet liked that a lot.

But when the chips were down and Chet was transferred to Palm Beach, he brushed aside Marcia's worries about her work. We heard all about it because we were consultants to Chet's company.

"No problem with the wife," he said breezily. "I just told her: if you're so crazy about your job, you can stay in New York. Or you can quit and come with me. So she quit. I guess I won that one."

Did he? We heard the next installment a few years later. Marcia did quit her department store job. But she soon found another outlet for her energy. Florida has a flourishing sportswear industry, and Marcia opened her own buying office, supplying Florida sportswear to small shops across the country.

She did not do too well. And Chet was not, to say the least, supportive. When Marcia was forced to close up shop, Chet breathed a sigh of relief. "Well," he told friends, "that's the end of this career business. Maybe she's finally got some sense into her head and come home."

Marcia came home, but not to Chet. She divorced him and is now once again in business, backed by her new husband, a Florida dress manufacturer in his seventies. She also has custody of the children. Chet has decided women are no damn good. He dates twenty-five-years-olds, but will probably not marry again.

Who won and who lost? You decide. We give up.

In fairness to men there are women who play the strong-arm game too. Phyllis Randall was one. Phyllis was a highly placed executive in a cosmetics company. Phyllis's husband, Ralph, was a computer scientist, who, even though he was a tenured professor at his university, earned slightly less than Phyllis. Their children were in college.

The combination worked nicely until Phyllis was asked to transfer. Ralph didn't want to move, but Phyllis overrode him. "I can't turn this job down," she said. "Have you any *idea* how much money there is to be made in the cosmetics business? And this transfer means I'll be in the Philadelphia home office where the action is.

"I know you've got tenure, but it's just not bringing in the money that this move will mean. You'll be able to find work, you've always talked about the demands for computer scientists. There have to be plenty of computer jobs in Philadelphia."

"Maybe you should go without me," said Ralph.

"Go without *you*! I couldn't live without you! Just look for a job. Please, just look."

Ralph looked. There were slim pickings for a man of his age and seniority in the new location. He did find an appropriate job with a research outfit. "But it's temporary," he warned Phyllis. "Depending on whether or not their grant comes through."

"Ralph, I know its rough but if this doesn't come through something else will. I wish you'd believe in yourself the way I do."

It Didn't Work

Things don't always come through. And so, a year after the move, Ralph was still conscientiously looking for a job but to no avail. His resumé was impressive, his credentials impeccable. "Overqualified," said those employers who were aware of laws against age discrimination. "Too old," said the honest ones.

"Never you mind," said his ever loving Phyllis. "What do we need money for? I'm making plenty for both of us. You just stay home and take it easy, or start working on the book you've always talked about writing."

"It's more than just the money, I don't think you understand how I really feel. I just can't face people or live with myself being unemployed."

Out of the blue came a telegram from a midwestern university, offering him a professorship in computer science.

"You're not going to take it!" said Phyllis.

"Oh yes, I am," said Ralph. "Of course, I'd want you to come along. There are plenty of jobs for cosmeticians in Michigan. You could open your own beauty shop. Or maybe this time you could stay home and write the book." End of discussion.

Ralph took his job, Phyllis kept hers. They live in separate cities. They still believe they have a marriage, but it seems to be dying of malnutrition. Ralph is making, slowly, a new group of friends based on his job. Some of them are women academics. Phyllis is doing the same thing, seeing men with similar career interests.

Maybe at this point, sadly enough, divorce *is* the answer for Ralph and Phyllis. But who could make that judgment but them.

"This Isn't the Amy I Married"

Divorce almost was the answer for Art and Amy Arthurs. Art was an assistant plant manager in New Jersey. Amy was a copywriter at an advertising agency in New York and in line for a better job as copy chief. Art knew how much she loved her job and was hesitant about taking a transfer to a small Texas town where there was not likely to be an advertising agency; certainly it wouldn't be a world renowned one, as was the company Amy worked for.

But Amy had always been so competent, and flexible! Art assumed she'd accept the move, pull herself together like she always had in the past and find a new job. However, a month before the move when the Arthurs came to our workshop Amy hadn't pulled herself together nor had she done much about finding a job. "There's something wrong here," a frustrated and angry Arthur expressed to the group during one of our relocation workshops. "All she does is mope and cry and she hasn't done a damn thing about finding a new job. She's acting like a whole different person. This isn't the Amy I married."

Amy snapped, "I didn't come to this workshop for any career counseling or marriage counseling or whatever it is you people do. I came in to explain to you what happens to wives in this corporation."

"What does?" she was asked.

"Well," said Amy, "take me, for example. Art and I were married in the fifties. I had a B.A., he was just back from Korea and had the GI Bill. So I stayed home, typed his papers, washed his socks and raised babies, while he finished up at MIT.

"Then Art signed on with the company and we moved to Chicago. I still worked. I got a job writing copy for a department store. The other wives thought this was funny—that was the fifties, and they were all into volunteer things. But I didn't care. I was good at my job, and I liked it.

"Of course, it all ended when we were transferred to a New England town. But I didn't give up. I sold a few articles to magazines about child raising, and on the strength of that I got my very own "Dear Amy" column in the local paper. Not much—but a beginning.

"Well, seven years ago we were transferred to New Jersey, and I finally connected. I got a job as a copywriter with Yates and Yandy. If I do say so myself, I did well. I'm working on their top accounts, and they want to make me a copy chief. Now I find out we're getting moved to some godforsaken town in Texas. Well, what am I supposed to do? Start in all over again taking in typing? Or being Dear Amy for the local weekly?

"No thanks. I've had it! The other wives were right. Don't try to work if your husband is married to the company."

"You're angry," someone said.

"You bet I am," said Amy. "Wouldn't you be? I've tried and tried to make something of myself, but every time I get started at work I like, I have to give it up and move on. Sure, I could get a job in Texas, maybe writing for the Neiman Marcus catalog. Well, no thanks. This time I'm going to spend my days reading it."

Amy suddenly started to cry. She not only got a lot of support from the group but Art started to understand why she wasn't looking for a job, the first and most important step in the Arthurs resolving their impasse.

MAKING IT IN DOUBLE HARNESS

We're assuming that two-career couples reading this chapter *want* to stay married. Certainly one quick and easy answer to career conflict is a quick and easy divorce, and quite a few young people faced with relocation do take this route.

As did many dedicated career women of the past. That's right. In the early years of the century women who seriously wanted to work either did not marry or if they did marry they usually got out fast. Margaret Sanger, Margaret Mead, Agatha Christie, Claire Booth Luce, to name a few luminous names, all had short-lived early marriages. Eleanor Roosevelt would probably have had such a marriage, too, if her husband had not been president.

But in those days the social climate was different. The disastrous first marriages of this generation of women were almost always to men typical of their time, and in their time women's place was unquestionably in the home. Men could accept a spinster doctor, teacher, or lawyer, but they couldn't tolerate similar ambitions in their own wives.

Can two-career couples make it today? Yes—if they really want to work at it.

If the husband's job is clearly more important to all concerned than the wife's, the wife adjusts.

But what if the two careers are more or less equally important? He's a sales executive, she's not a student but a tenured professor. He's a doctor, she's a lawyer. Or they're both executives at about the same level for different companies, or worse yet, for the same company.

One solution which Carolyn Bird writes about in her book *The Two Paycheck Marriage* calls for "supercool couples." It's the commuter marriage. He works in one city, she in another. They have apartments or houses in both places and meet there on weekends. These marriages, few and far between, usually work only for highly placed middle-aged couples with grown children. Or for the very young who have not yet started a family. For the in-betweens there's always a difficult decision to be made.

Such a couple might start the decision-making by each taking the job evaluation tests spelled out in chapter 2.

Hal and Hannah Nelson did—and discovered that Hal had about had it as an executive. He was ready to cash in his stock options and start his own small business. So Hannah accepted a job transfer, and Hal went into business for himself in the new city.

Clay and Cora Bremmer did the opposite. When Clay was transferred from the southeast, Cora quit her job as chief of pediatrics at a big city hospital and fulfilled a dream she'd always had. She finally took the long overdue plunge and went into private practice.

Too many variables are involved to list all the possible solutions. But two factors definitely should be considered: the family lifestyle and the children's feelings on the matter. The two career family might well turn back to chapter 6 and repeat the family conference plan outlined there. The only difference being that the discussion starts out, "Mom has a wonderful job opportunity . . ." Remember: the children are not there to vote. They're there to voice their opinions on the move and help mom and dad come to some sort of decision (parents should have veto power).

When parents can't quite decide whose job takes precedence, hearing out the kids can often clarify the picture. Whether dad or mom is the transferee, moving is still a family affair.

THE DISPLACED WIFE

When the husband's job takes automatic precedence, as it still does in most cases, it's quite possible for the working wife to find a satisfying job for herself in the new location. Here's how.

First, check out your husband's company. A number of major corporations, aware that the wife's job is an obstacle to relocation for male employees, have made a decision to help those wives find jobs. If your husband's company is doing this, by all means get your resumé to the appropriate department—fast.

Meanwhile, set up your own job hunting campaign. Are there companies in the new location you'd like to work for and who could use your skills? Fire off letters and resumés, just as you would if you were seeking a first job.

Of course, your skills can make an enormous difference. Professional women from doctors to cosmeticians usually have little trouble transferring their licenses to practice from one state to another. Lawyers are the outstanding exception; since state laws differ, lawyers generally have to take the bar exam all over again in a new state. Public school teaching certainly sounds like a portable profession. The problem is that school systems are reluctant to hire a teacher who may be transferred again in a few years. Substitute teaching in the public schools is a viable idea for the short-term transferred wife. And private school teaching is always a possibility. No graduate degrees are required. Salaries are lower, but the rules are more flexible.

General advice for all licensed professional women: check with the state board that issued your license for the applicable interstate regulations.

SKILLS THAT TRAVEL NICELY

In this category it's easiest to find a new job. Typists, technicians, accountants, data processors fit most easily into the job front anywhere. A resumé blitz plus inquiries at employment agencies and even the state employment bureau can pay off quickly. A possible obstacle facing wives with such skills is any large scale unemployment at the new location. If they're laying off assembly line workers, watch out.

But don't give up. If you're skilled *somebody* needs you. A tip: Kelly Services (formerly Kelly Girls) is no longer dealing in temporary clerical help only. They have over 100 job listings for men and women who're not clerk-typists. Some of the interesting openings for unskilled or semiskilled women call for receptionists, payroll clerks, door-to-door survey takers, comparison shoppers. True, the Kelly jobs are temporary—but temporary sometimes leads to permanent. Check out Kelly Services in the phone book.

IT'S NOT WHAT YOU KNOW

It's an old adage, but it's still true. When you're job seeking in a new location, take advantage of every connection you have.

Consult any friends and acquaintances in the new area.

Write to any national organization to which you belong: alumni clubs, religious groups, sorority affiliations, Hadassah or the Home Furnishing League—whatever is your social, professional or special interest. If you belong to the Sierra Club, by all means let the members in the new location know you're coming.

This is not the same as *applying for a job.* It's introducing yourself to people who may know people who may have a job for you.

Men have done this for years. Males seem to be born knowing that social or semisocial connections lead to contacts that eventually lead to jobs.

Recently, women are discovering it too. A new concept among job oriented women—or at least a new name for an old concept—is *networking.* It simply means joining already established women's groups or forming new organizations in which like-minded women can meet, get to know each other, discuss jobs and job problems and help each other start careers or further those already started.

Some such groups are long established—the Women's Forum, in New York, for example, or the American Association of University Women. Some are professionally oriented —the Electrical Women's Round Table, for example, or New York's Fashion Group. Many are brand new and started by enterprising women in communities all over the country to help any woman starting out on a career.

Kate Rand Lloyd, editor of *Working Woman* magazine, says: "The 'network' groups, old and new, are especially useful to wives of transferred men who're job hunting in a new location. They serve the same function in a business context as Newcomers Clubs do in a social context. We get many letters at *Working Woman* from relocated wives who have plugged into the job scene through 'women's network' groups."

MOVERS AND SHAKERS

For most of the individuals and families we counsel, the problems that emerge in a family move are pretty clear cut or they become so after a brief, clarifying discussion. Yet sometimes transferees discover that they're fighting chimeras, that the problem they think they're dealing with is not their problem at all.

This happened to the people profiled here, such as Anne Alexander, who flatly refused a group move to Tampa, Florida because, she said, "I could never leave Milwakuee."

On the face of it, it didn't make too much sense. Anne was thirty-five, divorced and had a thirteen-year-old son. She had neither a family nor a great many friends outside the company in Milwaukee, and the Florida job was a distinct step upward for her. Still, she was so adamant in her refusal to move that she refused even to make an exploratory trip.

At a group workshop, Anne was challenged by her colleagues. "What," one man wanted to know, "is so great about Milwaukee that you can't leave it?"

Anne floundered for an answer. Finally she admitted that it wasn't so much that she was attached to Milwakuee, but that she couldn't bear the thought of Florida.

"Why not?" her questioner wanted to know. Anne looked about in embarrassment. A number of her co-workers were a good deal older than she, yet she finally blurted out, "I'm not quite ready for the old folks home."

It developed that Anne believed that except for Palm Beach and Miami Beach and the Everglades, Florida was one enormous geriatric community, that she would meet no one her own age.

She also envisaged it as flat, arid and treeless, with wall to wall trailer camps.

"Where did you get *that* idea?" asked a woman who had visited the new location.

"Well, I've heard enough about Florida to *know*," Anne remarked huffily.

The other members of the group tried to set her straight or at least to persuade her to make an exploratory trip before she made up her mind.

Anne did and found a charming house in a wooded area very like the house she had in Milwaukee. Most of her neighbors were about her own age. She did spot one or two wheelchairs, but more bicycles and baby carriages. And the school system, she discovered, was excellent.

Anne had been about to turn down an excellent job on the basis of a fantasy that had no roots in fact. Many transferees do this; they've "heard" all about New York, or Mississippi, or Seattle, or wherever and close their minds to new information.

You can miss out on some good jobs that way. Give the new place a chance.

THE PROFESSIONAL VOLUNTEER

Alice Lindstrom was not, she told us with some vehemence, one of those women who insisted on having some sort of a career.

"Maybe I'm old fashioned," she said. "But I feel that if a woman can contribute to society by volunteer work, there's no need to take a job away from someone who really needs it. My husband has always been able to support us, so I've concentrated on volunteer work—and done very well at it." She recited a very impressive list of credentials—the church groups she had founded, the charity drives she had organized, the various organizations she had headed in the many communities she had lived in. Alice seemed to have a natural ability to get elected president of just about every group she joined.

"You could call me," she said, "a professional volunteer."

Then what was the problem?

"This *town* is the problem," she said. "I wasn't really crazy about moving here, but of course it was the opportunity Mort has been working for for twenty years. The company president *insisted* he take the job. 'We need new blood,' were his exact words. And of course Sam Mortimer, the man he's replacing, *has* been around for a long time.

"So I agreed to come. There's a very active chapter of my alumnae association here and of course the Girl Scouts—I've worked for them for years. I thought, well, there's plenty for an old pro like me to do but . . .

"But there wasn't," she said. "I mean, the women in this town simply don't know what they're doing. The Girl Scout Advisory Board is a *joke*. I went to one meeting—talk about *disorganized*!

"And the president of my alumnae association is this *girl* of thirty-two.

"I don't know what to do," she said. "It sounds crazy to complain that I'm too old to get a job when I never had a job in the first place, but that's what's happened.

"So what do I do now? Retire at fifty-five and play canasta all day?"

We didn't think Alice was crazy. She did have a problem and she knew it.

"It's not just that *I'm* dissatisfied," she said. "It's that I'm getting crankier by the day. I *know* I'm getting on Mort's nerves and right now with his new job he needs all the support he can get, not a resentful wife."

"Who are you resentful of?" we asked.

"These idiot women," she said. "And, well, maybe Mort, too, for bringing me here. Oh, I don't know. I'm all mixed up."

"Tell us again," we said, "why your husband was brought in at age fifty-six to replace Sam Mortimer."

"Because the company needed his experience. You know, there's no substitute for twenty-five years on the job."

There was a long silence.

"Oh," she said. "You mean the Girl Scouts and the alumnae association . . ."

"Exactly," we said.

"You're right, I guess," she said slowly. "I guess the young women need and want their chance, just as Mort wants his."

After a few counseling sessions Alice began to realize that a career in volunteer work differs little from a career in business.

Alice, at first, tried starting all over at the lowest rung of the ladder, volunteering for envelope addressing and other "gofer" chores in organizations headed by much younger women. She looked about desultorily for a job but she lacked the required experience. She tried taking courses, but Alice never was one for sitting back and listening.

After that, we didn't hear from Alice for a few months. When we did, she was very pleased with herself.

"I did what you said," she said. "I sat down and assessed exactly what I am good at, and it's *organizing* things. Well! This town badly needs a new library, so my partner and I are starting a fund raising drive to build one."

"Who's your partner?" we asked.

"As a matter of fact," said Alice, "it's my next door neighbor."

UP SCALE, DOWN SCALE

George Denehy is everything a good salesman is supposed to be—witty, affable, gregarious. He is not the world's most enlightened man, yet it came as a shock to his employers and his wife Peg when he turned down a transfer (with a promotion to assistant sales manager and a substantial raise) to the home office in New York.

"I don't know what's got into him," Peggy said. "He just won't face facts.

"First, we need the money. We *still* have two more kids to put through college. Besides that, George is fifty-one. This is make or break time for him. He *says* he can quit any time and get a better job with the competition. Merritt Manufacturing has been after him for years. But those years were a few years back. They're hiring the younger men now. Meanwhile, the Pfister pension plan is excellent, and it's not too many years before we'll be needing it."

George's version of the situation was different. "I know Peg has been telling you all about the pension plan and how I'm too old to get another job selling. Who knows, she may be right. But she left out one thing: where are we supposed to live?"

The Denehy's, it turned out, were living in a spacious, turn of the century house in a Chicago suburb. It had been a white elephant when they bought it twenty years ago for $35,000. They had paid off the low-rate mortgage years ago.

"Six bedrooms," said George, "and a beautiful garden. Kathleen and Mary Margaret were both married there. And plenty of space for parties, especially after we remodeled the kitchen. It was Peg's dream house when we bought it, and it's still our dream come true now.

"Women don't understand these things," he continued, "but you must know the real estate picture now. Even with the raise, I can't afford to move to New York. I'll go back on the road carrying sample cases before I'll have my Peggy living in a slum."

So persuasive was George's sales pitch that he almost had us crying our eyes out until we snapped him (and ourselves) back to reality.

We got out pencils and paper and helped George calculate the cost of relocating to a more expensive area, against the benefits involved in the move. (We show you how to do this, too, in chapter 12).

The result: George discovered that he could afford to move to a suburb of New York, within easy commuting distance. Their new house was smaller than the Chicago place, but that would have its advantages, too. The mortgage rate was relatively steep but easily affordable.

"Of course," said George, "it only has three bedrooms but then the kids are off and married now except for Michael and Eileen, and its not long for them. The garden isn't much, but there's a finished basement. And the plumbing works, which is more than I can say for the old house. It'll do nicely for us now. And when Peg and I retire, think of the parties we can give!"

Old salesmen never die: they just learn to readjust.

THE SCHIZOID

When Dwight and Dora Robertson consulted us, it was not because of any problems of their own, or so they maintained. It was because of their fourteen-year-old son Jeremy who had, since the family had been transferred to Connecticut six months ago, begun to change radically.

"We're really worried about him," Dwight said. "He's always been a perfectly normal kid. Back in Houston where he was born he had lots of friends, did well in school, liked sports—the all American boy. Two years ago, we were transferred to L.A., and he adapted very well.

"But suddenly he's changed completely. He gets terrible grades in school, has made no friends and hangs around the house all the time watching TV. That is, most of the time. A while back, he took to going out evenings, saying he was going to the movies with friends. Well, that seemed like a step in the right direction, till we found some pot in his raincoat pocket. The 'friends,' it turned out, were some of the town boys who hang around the local pizza joint and get into all kinds of trouble. We had a big row about that, and his excuse for everything is that he hates Connecticut."

"Of course, I can understand that," Dora said. "We're not crazy about Connecticut ourselves. It's not L.A., and its certainly not Houston. The people are snobbish, and it costs a lot to live here. On the other hand, the public schools are excellent. They have all kinds of sports programs, and Jeremy has the opportunity to meet really nice kids. We're the ones who should be complaining, not him."

"You're not facing facts, Dora," said Dwight. "There's definitely something wrong with Jeremy.

"I thought it was just laziness or lack of discipline on our part, but then the school guidance counselor called us in last week and gave us a lot of double talk about what happens to kids in adolescence. The upshot of it all is that he thinks Jeremy is a schizoid personality. What does that mean? That we should put him in an institution?"

A schizoid personality is someone unable, for any number of reasons, to function effectively in society. It's a catch-all term. It can be applied to harmless eccentrics and hermits; the little old lady who lives up the street and collects cats; the legendary Collyer brothers who lived with tons of newspapers and refuse. It can also be applied to the criminally insane—the nice quiet boy who is good at his studies and kind to his mother and then, one day, for no apparent reason, mounts a church tower and opens fire on the townspeople with a submachine gun.

It was, we thought, a mighty strong term to apply to Jeremy.

"Why not have him come in for a talk with us," we said.

Jeremy did come in. He was a friendly, initially rather shy boy, who opened up very quickly when we assured him we wanted to hear what *he* thought the problem was. He was apologetic about his grades and frankly frightened at the estimate of him given by the guidance counselor.

"I don't know what I'm doing wrong," he said. "I know I haven't made any friends, but then, how can I? Connecticut is really an awful place."

"What makes you think so?" we asked.

"My mom and dad said so," he said. "Just ask them. If they can't get along here, how can I?"

A good question. We had more sessions with the senior Robertsons and with Jeremy, and what was happening was what we suspected was happening. Dwight and Dora had made up their minds not to like Connecticut before they were transferred. They'd been happy in Houston, satisfied in Los Angeles, but the Connecticut move came unexpectedly. They had accepted it because it was a truly important career move for Dwight—but, as Dora said, "That doesn't mean we have to like it."

We asked them if they had made any effort to make friends, join groups or otherwise integrate themselves into life in the new location. Dwight admitted that they hadn't, but what had that to do with Jeremy's problems?

"Like father, like son," we suggested, and Dwight began to get the idea.

Jeremy's rejection of the new location did not spring from any internal problems of his own. He too had been happy in Houston and satisfied in L.A. The move to Connecticut had been a shock to him, too. His parents were acting out their unhappiness by behaving in an antisocial way, refusing to join the church and making no effort to make friends. Jeremy, in his behavior at school, was acting out his unhappiness in the same way. He was simply adopting the attitude of his parents. Except that, for Dwight and Dora, there was no handy guidance counselor to tell them they were "schizoid."

We kept meeting with the Robertsons, singly and as a family. The upshot of it all was that Dwight and Dora agreed to give Connecticut a chance. They joined the Congregational Church and went to Newcomers. Dora volunteered for the Hospital Committee and found, to her surprise, some women friends that she liked. Dwight offered to coach Little League baseball and was quickly taken up on the offer. Both became active members of the PTA.

"You know," Dwight reported to us several months later, "Connecticut isn't so bad, once you get to know people. I mean, we're going to be living here for a while so we might as well enjoy it."

And Jeremy? By this time, Dwight and Dora had almost forgotten about Jeremy's problems. Primarily because they had gradually disappeared. His grades began to improve. He began to make friends among the children of his parents' new friends. He wasn't the greatest player on his father's Little League team, but he showed up for batting practice.

The last time we spoke to him, he *denied* that he had ever disliked Connecticut. "Well, he said, "maybe I *thought* I did when we first came here, but it's really a great place. My mom and dad have made a lot friends here, and so have I."

MIXED DOUBLES

Ellen Randloph and Martha Ann Scott were both born in Georgia within a few miles of each other (as it turned out later). Both of their fathers were ministers. Both were honor students at school and went north to college—Ellen to the University of Chicago and Martha Ann to Oberlin. Both majored in political science with the idea of going into government or law. Instead, both married shortly after graduation. That was back in 1964.

Today they're corporate wives. Their husbands, Jay Randolph and Sam Scott, are southerners turned northerners too. Both are research scientists for the same New England pharmaceutical company. Both couples have been moved a lot. Both couples have high school aged children. The husbands have work interests in common. The wives have the problem of "Should I or shouldn't I have a career of my own?" The couples pal around a lot as a foursome.

This certainly isn't unusual, except that the Randolphs are black and the Scotts are white.

It doesn't happen all the time. We chose the example of the Randolphs and Scotts to dramatize the fact that mobility makes for a cosmopolitan outlook. It also helps, rather than hinders, the dream that all Americans pay lip service to, but few subscribe to in everyday life. Ethnic groups, transplanted by choice or by force to the new world, have not up to now given up much of their ethnic indentity.

This was pointed out in a much acclaimed book called *Beyond the Melting Pot* by Nathan Glazer and (now Senator) Daniel Patrick Moynihan. "The point about the melting pot," the authors write, "is that it did not happen."

The words inscribed on the base of the Statue of Liberty, "give me your poor . . ." embody a noble idea of the nineteenth century; immigrants seeking a new life in a new country would somehow be transformed into homogenized Americans shortly after steaming into New York harbor. It didn't happen that way. Many of the poor, once they got here, clung together and reinforced ethnic solidarity.

Glazer and Moynihan predicted that the erosion of ethnic differences was not likely in the forseeable future. But that prediction dates back almost two decades, and they were presuming a sedentary population.

The melting pot is beginning to happen, at least among the mobile population. As transferred families move from community to community, they cannot help but get to know people of other religions, other national backgrounds, and they discover that they have much more in common with their new neighbors than they had suspected.

"I'm a Polish Catholic," says Anna Dvorska, "and in my neighborhood the Polish Catholics stuck together. God forbid you should mix with Protestants or Jews or even Irish or Italian Catholics."

"I'm a Jew," said Ben Schwartz, "and although my parents were pretty broad-minded, the first thing my grandmother wanted to know if I dated a girl was 'Is she Jewish?'"

Today, both Anna and Ben, veteran corporate transferees, count among their friends Catholics, Protestants and Jews, along with some atheists and Buddhists, and people with ancestors from just about every part of the world.

We were nevertheless most interested in exploring this subject with the Scotts and the Randolphs, since the deepest ethnic split in contemporary culture is between blacks and whites. And, supposedly at least, between southern blacks and whites.

Ellen and Martha Ann were glad to fill us in.

"When I came north to school," Martha Ann said, "I didn't have any black friends at all. As a matter of fact, I hardly had *any* friends who weren't white Protestants. Well, school changed all that for me. I got to know people of *all* different backgrounds and made lots of good friends. After I married, we moved back down south, to Atlanta. I felt sort of let down. The company was run by southerners just like ourselves, and they hired in their own image. And after living up north for a while—well, I found the good old boys sort of dull."

"I made white friends in school, too," said Ellen. "But I always had the feeling that they were being nice to me *because* I was black. I remember when one of the girls in my dorm set me up with a blind date. 'You'll just *love* him,' she said. 'He looks exactly like Harry Belafonte.'

"When Jay went to work for Allied Pharmaceutical, I admit I was scared. What was it going to be like for a black woman to be a wife in a very conservative company?

"Well, I did make a lot of friends, but they were all black. The company, in response to Title VII of the Civil Rights Bill, was making an all-out effort to hire blacks, and we were among them. What happened was what you'd expect. The blacks stuck together and the whites stuck together. I belonged to a black women's discussion group. We had talks and discussion on black history, the importance of black solidarity and similar issues. These things are important, of course, but they're not all of life. My husband used to tease me about the group—he called it 'the corporate wives ghetto.' Because while we were learning the importance of our own culture, we were cutting ourselves off from others.

"Then Jay was transferred to Tulsa. And this time it wasn't because of Title VII, but because of the important research he had done on a new product the company was developing. There weren't many blacks there, and we gradually found ourselves socializing with white neighbors and co-workers.

"By the time we got to Tulsa, I was pretty comfortable with white people and then I met Martha Ann. Well, as soon as I heard her accent, I was right back in Gainsville, Georgia. Northerners, I was used to by now, even easterners and westerners. But a white southerner was something else.

"Yet it all happened very naturally. We met at Newcomers, and found out we came from towns ten miles apart. When they had a covered dish supper—well, Martha Ann's beef and bean stew sure tasted like home. We both joined the Methodist Church and got involved in helping start a day care center. In the 1976 election it turned out we were the only wives who supported Jimmy Carter.

"What finally did it was when Jay and I drove out to a suburb to a little jazz club in the area to hear Earl Hines. The place was jammed with students, but right up there, hanging over the piano, were Martha Ann and Scott. As practically the only adults in the place, we took a table together, and from then on things just took their natural course.

"Martha and I have talked a lot about how being forced to transfer has pretty much freed us of all our ethnic prejudices—except maybe one."

"What's that?" we asked.

The two women giggled. "Don't spread it around," Martha Ann said, "but we don't really like Yankees very much."

MARJORIE, THE WINNER

Marjorie Miller is not (never has been and never will be) a client of ours. We have saved her story for last, because in her lifetime of sixty-seven years, she has suffered all the problems and pleasures of mobility and come out a definite winner.

We met Marjorie in the delightful house she shares with her second husband Max on the west coast of Florida. She is, she says, "sort of retired, but not really. I don't imagine I ever will.

"Don't try to tell me about moving," she said, over a glass of sherry on her beautifully planted patio. "I guess I've moved more than anybody in the history of the world—male or female.

"Oh, I hated it when I started out," she said. "When my first husband Theo and I were first married his company moved him from West Hartford to South Norwalk. Debbie was a baby, Sarah wasn't born yet. Well, I can remember sitting in this empty house in South Norwalk with an infant child, no heat and no furniture. The movers were supposed to show up that day and they didn't till the following night. Theo was off at a sales meeting. What did I do? I lit candles, wrapped Debbie and me up in blankets, and cried my eyes out.

"After that, it got easier. I learned the ropes of moving. A good thing too, for the next fifteen years we were moved all over the United States, and to Switzerland and to England.

"I knew then that moving was going to be our way of life, so I decided to make the best of it. Oh certainly, there were some fiascos. At one point, Theo changed jobs and we were up against it financially. That was, as I recall, in Milwakuee. Fortunately I'm trained as a home economist, so I got a job as a hospital dietitian, and that helped tide us over.

"Debbie and Sarah? I think we moved so much that they thought people who didn't move were peculiar. My philosophy and Theo's was that every place we settled down, we made the most of. We went out of our way to make friends, even though we knew we wouldn't keep them long. And the girls followed the pattern.

"The greatest setback I had was ten years ago when Theo died. Heart attack. Deb and Sarah were married by then—Debbie to a doctor, Sarah to a naval officer—but I suddenly felt very old and left out. I had a job by then as a dietitian in a hospital in Atlanta, but with Theo gone, I just didn't want to stay. So I decided that, as a widow with no responsibilities and a small income I'd do what I knew best—move.

"I considered all the possibilities of retirement. I didn't really want to work any more, and I could afford not to. And I didn't want to be a burden on Debbie and Sarah. Both of them were pleading with me to move in with them but that never would have worked.

"So I took a cruise to get my head together. On the cruise I ran into a couple I had met years ago in England. They talked me into going back to work. Not as a home economist though. It developed that they owned a hotel on an island in the Caribbean and needed someone to take over as executive assistant to the new president, their son.

"I've always loved the islands. And this seemed to be an ideal solution to my immediate problem. And so I took the job.

"At the hotel I met Max who was also widowed. He came down every year and the third time round, he asked me to marry him. By that time my assistant at the hotel was well able to take over my job, so Max and I were married and moved one more time—back to the states. And here we are, enjoying the Florida life."

Did Marjorie intend to move again? "Not if I have anything to say about it," said Max. "No, I guess I'm settled for life," said Marjorie. "But life here is anything but dull. Debbie, Sarah and the grandchildren visit regularly. And so does Max's family. We're kept busy just changing the sheets in the guest rooms."

"Tell about your cookbook," Max prompted.

"It's just a little paperback called *Home Cooking, USA,*" Marjorie said. "My favorite recipes from all the places I've lived. It's published by a little Florida company. The big thrill came when I was asked to go on a trip around the country to promote it on television."

"Except they wouldn't pay your expenses," said Max.

"Well, yes," said Marjorie. "But it didn't really matter. There wasn't a city they sent me to where I didn't have good friends I could stay with. After all, I'd lived in most of them."

We had no advice to give Marjorie about moving. But she had some advice for us.

"Tell all your clients who are unhappy about being transferred a lot that it can be a great life if you learn the rules. Sure I've had unhappy times. I've felt badly about leaving old friends in one city, but my philosophy was to keep in touch and meanwhile make new friends in the next place. The girls got used to it early in life and for them it was a good experience—especially Sarah; she's now a Navy wife.

"When I was widowed, if I'd been afraid to move, I never would have met Max. I'd probably be a retired hospital employee on a tiny pension. Instead, I have a whole new exciting life. I firmly believe that keeping moving may be a lot of headaches at first but it keeps you young. It terrifies me to think where I'd be today if I'd never left West Hartford!"

C H A P T E R

12

MONEY TRUTH AND THE MONEY CONSEQUENCES

Take this depressingly typical scenario. The combatants are employer and employee. The losers: both.

John Coates, the president of a very successful tool company, has two plants, one in Long Island and the other in Bergen County, New Jersey. John makes the decision to promote Dick Spencer to plant manager in New Jersey, with a substantial raise.

John's company rarely moves people, so John is not familiar with how much it costs an employee to relocate, nor is he familiar with the substantial relocation benefits that companies with high transfer activity routinely ante up these days. John assumes that Dick's raise will more than offset moving costs and that Dick will jump at the opportunity.

Dick has lived in the same Long Island house for fifteen years and has a relatively low monthly mortgage payment. Although houses in his community appreciate slowly, and Dick has continually been advised to "buy up," Dick loves his ability to live within his means and save slowly but steadily.

Two days after John was offered his promotion he turned it down.

"Why?" cried an incredulous John.

"I spoke to some people and they said houses in Bergen County are out of sight, John. I just can't afford to move," said Dick.

John left the meeting surprised, puzzled and convinced that Dick must be scared to take the job. Dick, who desperately wanted the job, felt regret.

The point is that both the company and employee lose out when the financial consequences of a move to an employee are not clearly understood by both. John, unfamiliar with relocation costs and policies, was *unable* to make a fair offer to Dick. Dick really had no idea how to evaluate the financial consequences of the move and made his decision on one piece of information, which he got from some friends.

Even employees at large companies with highly sophisticated relocation policies sometimes have too little information to calculate the financial consequences of a relocation. This is *not* an automatic push-pull process. It requires a good deal of objectivity, and under the gun of a potential move, people become subjective, shortsighted and unable to do the kind of thinking required.

Many employees reject transfers for financial reasons when a full consideration of the facts might yield another decision. And employees sometimes accept a transfer to their financial detriment and then blame the company for taking advantage of them. Obviously, an objective, informed, understanding discussion of finances between employee and employer is crucial for everyone involved.

This chapter shows you step-by-step how to gauge the financial consequences of your potential transfer.

THE DOLLAR ITEMS TO THINK ABOUT

Four major financial aspects have to be thought about.

I. *Onetime costs.* All cost associated with selling, your old home, finding and buying a new one, and moving. For each, you must consider how much you will pay out of pocket and how much is covered by the relocation program of your company. It's essential to understand thoroughly the ins and outs of your company's program. One time costs may include the following items.

A. initial interview at a new job site
B. house hunting visits
C. sale of your present home
D. temporary living arrangements if permanent arrangements have not been completed at the time of relocation
E. shipment of household goods
F. transporting you and your family to the new location
G. home purchase and closing costs
H. duplicate housing costs, if unavoidable
 I. miscellaneous

II. *Tax ramifications.* If you work for a company that provides relocation benefits you need to be aware of the tax consequences. Generally, someone within the corporation is familiar with the tax aspects, but here are the basics to help you understand and calculate the tax conquences tc you, if relocation benefits are provided.

A. *House hunting and temporary living.* Reimbursements you receive for house hunting and temporary living are considered taxable income. You are, however, allowed a $1,500 exemption. If your temporary living time exceeds thirty days, all reimbursements from the thirty-first day on become taxable income if you have not exceeded the $1500 exemption.

B. *Home purchase and home disposition.*
    1. Reimbursements *you* receive from your company for costs associated with selling your old home and buying a new one are considered taxable income. Again, you're allowed a $1,500 exemption; any portion of the $1,500 exemption allowed for house hunting and temporary living that you have not used may be added to the total exemption allowed

for home disposition and home purchase. For example, if you were reimbursed $500 for house hunting, you have a $2,500 exemption from taxes for any reimbursements you receive for home purchase and home disposition.

2. If home disposition and home sale assistance is provided by your corporation through a relocation company (such as Homequity or Merrill Lynch) there is no taxable income to you. In this case your corporation pays a fee to the third party company for providing the service; they in turn handle the paperwork and costs associated with the sale of your old home and purchase of the new one. You're not directly reimbursed and therefore there is no taxable income to you.

C. *Shipment of household goods.* Reimbursements in this category are completely exempt from taxation.

D. *Moving trip.* Reimbursement for expenses incurred in moving you and your family from location A to location B is completely exempt from taxation.

E. *Cost of living differential.* Any salary increase, even if it's labeled "cost of living differential" or "area adjustment" is treated as gross income and is taxable.

F. *Mortgage interest differentials.* Any reimbursements for mortgage payments are treated as gross income and are taxable.

G. *Tax gross up.* Some corporations reimburse employees for the increase the employee pays in taxes due to the relocation benefits, which are considered taxable income. This reimbursement, known as a "tax gross up" is also considered taxable as gross income.

III. *Long-term expenses.* This is the cost of living change caused by relocation. Companies traditionally have not helped much with this, but surges in interest rates and housing costs have led major companies to provide some assistance in recent years. Some companies, in addition to any merit increase triggered by a relocation, provide a cost of living salary adjustment based on some estimate of how costs in the new area compare to costs in the old location. With the dramatic upsurge in interest rates some large corporation provide "mortgage interest differentials." They calculate any increase in monthly mortgage payments at the new location and cover the difference, generally for one to three years. Since this is expensive, this benefit is only provided by very large corporations.

    A. Cost of living studies done by Runzheimer and Company, a management consulting firm headquartered in Rochester, Wisconsin, show that many costs such as food and medical care are generally the same across the country. Three items—taxes, transportation and housing—do vary widely and account for the major portion of cost of living differentials. Runzheimer says that these three factors make up 50–70 percent of the average family budget and account for over 80 percent of cost of living differentials.

    B. This general rule doesn't always hold true. If you're changing climates, the initial investment in clothes should be considered a one time expense and can sometimes be considerable. If you're moving to an area or neighborhood that is going to produce a change in life style, consider these costs. However, generally Runzheimer's guidelines are good and should help you accurately calculate cost of living differentials.

    C. You'll want to compare your current and projected cost in the new community for:
       1. Housing
       2. Taxes
       3. Transportation
    D. After that consider whether your company provides any benefits to cover differences that arise.

IV. *The big picture: cost vs. potential gains.* One time costs, tax ramifications and cost of living differentials must now be weighed against potential gains. Think in short as well as long range terms and consider:

A. Immediate salary increase.

B. Potential merit salary increases resulting from accepting the transfer. Although a transfer sometimes does not bring a significant salary increase it often greatly helps a career path and holds the potential for future increases.

C. Appreciation on real estate. Sometimes a more expensive area also is one with a high appreciation rate. Check with local brokers; look at sales figures for houses comparable to your area; get a good reading on the local market; and consider the appreciation rate as a potential gain. Consider buying a smaller house, if possible, and taking advantage of the appreciation rate. Don't make the mistake of assuming you you can't afford an area because you've heard it's too expensive. All localities, even expensive ones, have less expensive areas.

Below is a form entitled The Financial Consequences of Your Move. It's a step-by-step chart to help you go through the most objective analysis you can make of your move. Take the time to use it! Maybe that transfer you want but thought you couldn't afford is really to your advantage. Using the form will also help identify what you can afford in a new community and avoid the unfortunate mistake of buying over your head.

FINANCIAL CONSEQUENCES OF YOUR MOVE

Part 1—One time costs

1. Estimate the costs in each category applicable to your projected move and enter in the first column.

2. Place the amount of that cost covered by your company's relocation policy in the second column.

3. Write the amount of that cost that you will pay out of pocket in the third column.

4. Add up subtotals to get total one time cost.

	Cost	Covered by company	Cost to employee
1. *Initial interview*			
Transportation			
Lodging			
Meals			
ubtotal			
2. *Home search*			
Transportation			
Lodging			
Meals			
Rental Car			
Baby-sitting			
Subtotal			
3. *Home disposition*			
Real estate commission			
Mortgage prepayments penalty			
Attorney's and title fees			
Appraisals			
Home advertising fees			
Insurance			
Miscellaneous selling costs			
Subtotal			

Part 1—One time costs (continued)

	Cost	Covered by company	Cost to employee
4. Temporary living arrangements for employee and family			
Transportation			
Lodging			
Meals			
Incidentals			
Subtotal			
5. Shipment of household goods			
Packing			
Transportation			
Unpacking			
Storage			
Insurance			
Car/boat			
Subtotal			
6. Enroute to new location			
Transportation			
Lodging			
Meals			
Subtotal			

Part 1—One time costs (continued)

	Cost	Covered by company	Cost to employee
7. Home purchase and closing cost			
Attorney's fees			
Mortgage fees/bank appraisal			
Home inspection fees			
Survey costs			
Title search/title insurance			
Recording fees/transfer taxes			
Other			
Subtotal			
8. Duplicate housing costs			
Interest on bridge loan			
Insurance, utilities, maintenance			
Property taxes			
Repairs			
Improvements			
Miscellaneous carrying costs			
Subtotal			
9. Miscellaneous			
Subtotal			
Total of all one time costs			

FINANCIAL CONSEQUENCES OF YOUR MOVE

Part 2—Tax ramifications

1. Place your company's reimbursements for the items listed in the first column. Subtract exemptions where applicable.

2. Place the gross taxable income you will have as a result of your company's relocation benefits in the second column.

3. Use this figure to calculate the increased taxes, if any, you will pay as a result of this relocation.

Item Reimbursed	Amount	Gross taxable Income
1. House hunting trip and temporary living	−1,500 =	
2. Home disposition and home purchase costs	−1,500 =	
3. Mortgage interest differential (first year)		
4. Tax gross up		
	Total	

FINANCIAL CONSEQUENCES OF YOUR MOVE

Part 3—Long-term expense

1. Place the cost for the item listed at your current location in the first column.

2. Place the costs you project in your new community based on the type of home you expect to purchase and community you expect to live in in the second column.

3. Place the cost differential in the third column.

4. After this has been done, calculate the total cost-of-living differential in the indicated columns.

	Current monthly amount	Projected monthly amount in new community	Difference + or −
Housing			
Mortgage payment (principal and interest)			
Homeowners insurance			
Utilities			
Regular maintenance			
Real local property taxes			
Subtotal			
Taxes			
Federal			
State			
City			
Social security			
Sales tax			
Subtotal			
Transportation			
Public commutation			
Gas			
Oil			
Tires			
Depreciation			
Auto insurance			

Part 3—Long-term expense (continued)

	Current monthly amount	Projected monthly amount in new community	Difference + or −
Maintenance			
Repairs			
Finance charges			
Subtotal			

Total long-term expense

+ or − per month   × 12   = yearly difference

Housing			
Taxes			
Transportation			
Total long-term expense			

FINANCIAL CONSEQUENCES OF YOUR MOVE

Part 4—The big picture: cost vs. potential gain

Although there is no foolproof formula to help you look at the big picture, here are two helpful perspectives.

1. Calculate your current and projected net disposable income by subtracting the cost of living from salary.

2. Compare the already discussed costs with the potential long range gains. Don't be shortsighted; while a bird in the hand is worth two in the bush, with real estate and corporate salaries sometimes eight birds are in the underbrush.

	Current	Projected in new community
Employee salary		
Spouse salary		
Total		

Cost of living
(including taxes)

____

Net disposable income

____

| Costs | versus | Potential gain |

	Amount
One time costs	
Tax increase	
Long-term expense (for 1 year)	

Merit salary increase:

Real estate appreciation:

HOW THIS PROCESS CAN WORK FOR YOU

When Ray Floyd and his wife Amy came to a Transition, Inc., decision-making workshop they were uncertain whether to accept a relocation offered to Ray. Ray was twenty-seven and worked for a major corporation in Houston at a salary of $16,000. The company had a good relocation policy.

Amy, twenty-six, was earning $10,000 as an executive secretary. Two years ago, when they first got married, they were advised to take every cent they had and buy a home. Their parents helped them with the down payment, and they were able to purchase a 2,200 square foot house for $66,396 with a $55,313 mortgage at 11 percent. When they were offered the relocation they had their house appraised and it was valued at $73,750.

Although Ray and Amy had never moved before they were eager to accept the transfer. It meant a small raise; a good career step for Ray; and the Los Angeles area of California was very attractive to them. Both were active, adventurous, liked new experiences and outdoor living.

Their major concern was financial. "We've heard L.A. is just out of the question," said Amy, "and we're just about making it now. Ray's not being offered a big salary."

Ray was concerned, "I just don't know how to figure out what this damn thing's going to cost," he said. "I've gone to our company accountant for advice, and all he knows about are the tax laws. I spoke to our personnel manager last week, and she gave me sixteen forms. I looked through them for four hours last night. There's a lot of detail, but it still doesn't give me any idea which direction to go. L.A.'s so expensive I just don't think we can make this move."

We spent some time in the workshop with the Floyds and explained the principles of our suggested analysis. The couple was given the forms that you find on page 182. Here's what the Floyds finally came up with.

FINANCIAL CONSEQUENCES OF YOUR MOVE

(Filled out by the Floyds)

Part 1—One time costs

1. Estimate the costs in each category applicable to your projected move in the first column.

2. Place the amount of that cost covered by your company's relocation policy in the second column.

3. Write the amount of that cost that you will pay out of pocket in the third column.

4. Add up subtotals to get total one time cost.

		Cost	Covered by company	Cost to employee
1. *Initial interview*				
Transportation		138	0	138
Lodging		50	0	50
Meals		45	0	45
	Subtotal	233	0	233
2. *Home search*				
Transportation		380	380	0
Lodging		187	187	0

Part 1—One time costs (continued)

		Cost	Covered by company	Cost to employee
Meals		210	210	0
Rental Car		148	148	0
Baby-sitting		168	168	0
	Subtotal	1,093	1,093	0
3. Home disposition				
Real estate commission		3,770	3,770	0
Mortgage prepayments penalty		347	347	0
Attorney's and title fees		753	753	0
Appraisals		405	0	405
Home advertising fees		116	0	116
Insurance		0	0	0
Miscellaneous selling costs		290	0	290
	Subtotal	5,681	4,870	811
4. Temporary living arrangements for employee and family				
Transportation		270	270	0
Lodging		1,137	1,100	37
Meals		747	675	72
Incidentals		48	0	48
	Subtotal	2,202	2,045	157
5. Shipment of household goods				
Packing		373	373	0

Part 1—One time costs (continued)

		Cost	Covered by company	Cost to employee
Transportation		886	886	0
Unpacking		373	373	0
Storage		116	116	0
Insurance		52	52	0
Car/boat		401	401	0
	Subtotal	2,201	2,201	0

6. *Enroute to new location*

Transportation		156	156	0
Lodging		15	15	0
Meals		80	80	0
	Subtotal	251	251	0

7. *Home purchase and
   closing cost*

Attorney's fees		652	0	652
Mortgage fees/ bank appraisal		177	0	177
Home inspection fees		0	0	0
Survey costs		0	0	0
Title search/ title insurance		0	0	0
Recording fees/ transfer taxes		177	0	177
Other		0	0	0
	Subtotal	1,006	0	1,006

Part 1—One time costs (continued)

		Cost	Covered by company	Cost to employee
8. *Duplicate housing costs*				
Interest on bridge loan		521	521	0
Insurance, utilities, maintenance		173	0	173
Property taxes		464	464	0
Repairs		290	0	290
Improvements		290	0	290
Miscellaneous carrying costs		1,856	0	1,856
	Subtotal	3,594	985	2,609
9. *Miscellaneous*		1,000	1,000	0
	Subtotal	1,000	1,000	0
Total of all one time costs		$17,261	$12,445	$4,816

FINANCIAL CONSEQUENCES OF YOUR MOVE

Part 2—Tax ramifications

1. Place your company's reimbursements for the items listed in the first column. Subtract exemptions where applicable.

2. Place the gross taxable income you will have as a result of your company's relocation benefits in the second column. Use this figure to calculate the increased taxes, if any, you will pay as a result of this relocation.

Part 2—Tax ramificatations (continued)

Item Reimbursed	Amount			Gross Taxable Income
1. House hunting trip and home purchase costs	3,138	−1,500	=	1,638
2. Home disposition and temporary living	4,870	−1,500	=	3,370
3. Mortgage interest differential (1st year)	0			0
4. Tax gross up	0			0
			Total	$5,008

The Floyds benefits added $5,008 to their gross income for the year of the projected move. This meant they would pay $1,771 more in taxes that year.

FINANCIAL CONSEQUENCES OF YOUR MOVE

Part 3—Long-term expense

1. Place the cost for the item listed at your current location and enter in the first column.

2. Place the costs you project in your new community based on the type of home you expect to purchase and community you expect to live in in the second column.

3. Place the cost differential in the third column.

4. After this has ben done, calculate the total cost-of-living differential in the indicated columns.

	Current monthly amount	Projected monthly amount in new community	Difference + or −
Housing			
Mortgage payment (principal and interest)	537	636	+99
Homeowners insurance	25	24	− 1

Part 3—Long-term expense *(continued)*

	Current monthly amount	Projected monthly amount in new community	Difference + or −
Utilities	129	72	− 57
Regular maintenance	50	50	0
Real local property taxes	129	83	− 46
		Subtotal − 5	
Taxes			
Federal	394	417	+23
State	no change		0
City	no change		0
Social security	133	148	+15
Sales tax	no change		0
Subtotal	527	565	+38
Transportation			
Public commutation	25	56	+31
Gas	no change		0
Oil	no change		0
Tires	no change		0
Depreciation	no change		0
Auto Insurance	63	58	− 5
Maintenance	no change		0
Repairs	no change		0
Finance charges	no change		0
Subtotal	25	56	+26

Part 3—Long-term expense (continued)

Total long-term expense

	+ or − per month	× 12	= yearly difference
Housing	− 5	× 12	−60
Taxes	+38	× 12	456
Transportation	+26	× 12	312
Total long-term expense			$708

FINANCIAL CONSEQUENCES OF YOUR MOVE

Part 4—The big picture: cost vs. potential gain

Although there is no foolproof formula to help you look at the big picture here are two helpful perspectives.

1. Calculate your current and projected net disposable income by subtracting the cost of living from salary.

2. Compare the already discussed costs with the potential long range gains. Don't be shortsighted; while a bird in the hand is worth two in the bush, with real estate and corporate salaries sometimes eight birds are in the underbrush.

		Current	Projected in new community
Employee salary		$16,000	$18,000
Spouse salary		$10,000	$11,000
	Total	$26,000	$29,000
Cost of living (including taxes)		$24,500	$26,000
Net disposable income		$1,500	$ 3,000

Costs

	Amount	*Potential Gain*
One time costs	$4,816	Merit Salary Increase: 3,000/year
Tax increase	$1,770	Real Estate Appreciation: 15 percent/ year or $12,000 first year
Long-term expense (for 1 year)	$ 708	

WHAT HAPPENED TO THE FLOYDS

The day after our worshop, Amy Floyd called a good broker in Los Angeles to get some feel for housing costs. True, she was told prices in L.A. were sky high, but some surrounding communities were a little more reasonable. While prices there were high, too, some small houses were available in communities with appreciation hovering around 15 percent for three years.

That night Amy and Dick discussed their feelings about a smaller house and agreed it could meet their current needs. They decided to apply the idea of going through our step-by-step guide, using a house described to Amy on the phone that sounded suitable. Amy was assured by the broker that if this one was not to their liking there were many comparable ones at about the same price.

The house they considered was small, 1,700 square feet, but very attractive, well maintained and in an excellent neighborhood. The price was $86,500, and the Floyds figured on a $59,625 mortgage at 12.5 percent.

As you can see in Part 4, the Floyds discovered that to make the move they would pay $6,587 (including tax liability) out of pocket; their company would pay $12,445. With their decision to buy a smaller house they found that over the long haul their cost of living would not change much.

When they looked at their overall picture it was clear that the $6,000 out of pocket expense was relatively insignificant compared to the likely long range gains. The significance of the move for Ray's career insured him at least a $3,000 raise for the next two years. The appreciation on their house for the first year alone was going to be in the neighborhood of $12,000 compared to $3,000 in his old neighborhood. Ray was told by his manager that if he accepted this move and performed well he could expect to be moved again in three years. Ray's house would by then appreciate between $30,000 to $40,000.

The Floyds decision was easy.

NOT FOR MANAGERS ONLY (EMPLOYEES PLEASE LISTEN IN)

Relocation has become a big and delicate factor in American industry. Only a decade ago, relocation, frequently with the promise of promotion and raise, was accepted without question (or without too many questions) by most employees. As managers know only too well, this is no longer true, the reasons being complex and interrelated.

While the *number* of employee transfers has not changed appreciably, many moves today are *group* moves. An entire division—executives, technicans, typists and all—is often asked to relocate as a unit. The company, of course, pays moving expenses and attempts to take much of the hassle out of the process of relocation, but raises and promotions are not common and certainly not automatic. In a group move, employees are asked to pick up their jobs and themselves and their families and plunk them down in new territory.

With a tight housing market, relocation no longer means making a profit on the old house, as often happened in the old days. Today a transfer may mean taking a loss.

The growing number of two career families is another major new complication, as we've discussed earlier in this book. A number of surveys clearly indicate that corporations are getting more and more transfer turndowns because the spouse has a job that's too meaningful or financially rewarding (or both) to leave.

Managers are also aware that today's families are much more conscious of lifestyles. They're much more willing to move to an area where the climate and cultural advantages suit them, than to an area where they do not. And a lot of locations do not.

So even though relocation has become more and more essential to the rational operation of a successful business, more and more employees are reluctant to move or refuse outright to pull up stakes.

This is a tough dilemma for management.

First, there's the cost. It may cost perhaps $30,000 to $50,000 to transport an employee and family from location A to location B and resettle them. It can cost up to five times as much to find, train, and break in a replacement. In some cases, replacing employees who will not move to a new location could prove financially disastrous. It can take far too long to find the right person and to train him.

And then there's human cost to employer and employee alike—the massive disruptions, the wear and tear on everybody's nerves. It looks like an impossible situation to many managers, particularly the older generations; where are the old days when you hired 'em when you needed 'em and fired 'em when you didn't?

Younger managers, who have learned to live with trade unions and accept fringe benefits as a fact of business life, see it differently—but not much differently.

THE WAY DAN SEES IT

Dan Shortway is a senior vice-president in a middle-sized corporation. He is forty-seven, an enrolled Republican who often votes Democratic, and he considers himself a progressive thinker.

He is what most people would describe as a good and conscientious man. He believes that people and companies have to change with the times. He believes in meeting people half way.

"I've always understood labor's point of view," he says. "I used to have fights with my father about it when I was at Dartmouth. I believe that the laborer is worthy of his hire. And that's not Communism, as my father thought it was. It's good old Henry Ford Americanism. He knew what he was doing even way back when he saw that if you pay your workers five dollars a day—unheard of then—they can buy more Fords."

In his company Dan has been the executive with the best track record for settling union-management disputes. But then he was put in charge of relocation. And that became a new ball game for Dan.

Right now he's pretty discouraged. "I don't know what the answer is," he says.

"To give you an example, we recently moved a division of the company from Long Island to New Jersey.

"Now what the hell big difference is there between Long Island and New Jersey? It isn't as if we're deploying all hands to outer Siberia, for crying out loud! Nobody lost anything in terms of job status, money, benefits, you name it. And the move didn't cost them a cent!

"We have one of those relocation companies that not only finds them new houses or apartments or whatever; they'll even buy the old house giving the employee his equity right away. They take care of the move. They do everything but pick up the family bodily and carry them to the new location. At our expense, of course. And still, something like a third of them refused to go! Can you beat that?

"This makes me feel kind of helpless. For a whole lot of reasons. The union guys trust me, and now they think I've let them down. Besides that, a lot of the dropouts *won't* be able to find other jobs. I know that; they don't. But how do you reach them?

"Now that's your group move. The other problem is individual transfers, like an ambitious young guy who we think a lot of is offered a raise and promotion if and when he moves to a new location. That's the kind of thing I would grab like a shot—in fact, I have, many times. That's why I'm here today.

"But now I'm getting these young guys in here, twenty-eight, thirty years old, I tell 'em they're doing a terrific job and offer them a real opportunity with the company if they'll move. A promotion, a hefty raise and what goes with it—a sort of understanding that they're on our top priority list.

"It doesn't work! Half the time they flounder around making excuses and then come in and tell me they can't move because the wife doesn't want to go or their kids don't want to go, or the *dog* doesn't want to go, for pete's sakes!

"Some of them are cutting their own throats. A crack secretary can refuse to move and turn up with a shiny new job in a week. But a $35,000 executive who turns down relocation may find himself on unemployment for a long, long time.

"I'm telling you, I don't know what the answer is! Maybe there isn't any answer. People today just don't want to work or at least they don't want to work enough to make a few sacrifices.

"Maybe my father was right."

Not according to Peter F. Drucker, who is perhaps our leading authority on the sociology of business.

In an editorial page essay in the *Wall Street Journal* (March 4, 1980), Professor Drucker advanced the theory that jobs, rather than land or accumulated wealth, are today's most valued form of personal property.

His evidence is hard to argue with. *Ninety-three percent of all Americans* are employees of organizations, large and small. Whether they're union members, security minded technicians, ambitious trainees, executive vice-presidents or company presidents themselves, the job is central to their lives.

WHY A JOB ISN'T JUST A JOB

The job—at whatever level—provides or has the potential of providing:

1. A basic source of income.
2. A sense of mastery, competence and gratification.
3. The security of health and medical benefits and retirement plans.
4. A ready-made social life. Employees on all levels have the maximum opportunity to meet others like themselves; firm friendships often result. And even if they don't, the daily camaraderie of the office or the shop is a satisfying form of social life in itself.

Perhaps most important, there's identification with the organization. In our performance-conscious society, people are defined less and less according to where they came from or who their parents were, and more and more by what they *do*. And, not incidentally, for whom they do it.

Managers may find this hard to believe, but most employees take pride in and (if challenged) will defend *their* company. Rank and file office workers employed by big name corporations take enormous satisfaction in the prestige of their company and tend to preen themselves among their peers. The peers will often retaliate by describing the great product and the great future *their* company has, even if at this point the company is a six person operation that couldn't qualify for the Fortune Five Million.

True, these are the followers and not the leaders. But even the most militant of union representatives or most obstreperous of innovative vice-presidents usually has no quarrel with the institution of the company; just with the policies of those currently in control. They'd rather run it *their* way. It's a family fight.

For most employees, especially long-term employees, the company is a second family. And the depth of their affiliation, even kinship, is often underestimated by managers.

Employees who're reluctant to move or uncertain about it or refuse relocation outright are not, as Dan Shortway believes, lazy, irresponsible or disloyal to the company.

Dan Shortway has perceived that people now place equal importance on job, family and life style considerations. The error he made was to interpret these changing priorities to mean that his employees no longer cared about their jobs.

Quite the contrary. The reluctant long-distance mover is caught in a true identity crisis along with the practical problems that inevitably accompany a transfer. He or she is being forced to choose between the community he *belongs* to and the company he *belongs* to. It's not an easy choice.

For most, there is much that management can do to help resolve the dilemma. No manager can arrange for an employee to take his hometown along with him. But once he understands the employee's side of things, a manager can do much to help the employee realize that he *is* needed, wanted and understood by his company, and that it can help him create a hometown wherever he goes. It's not just a matter of money. It's a matter of communications.

MOTIVATING THE INDIVIDUAL TO MOVE

A manager assigned to inform an individual that he's being transferred must be aware that:

1. This information is bound to be unsettling. Even if an

employee's long-term dream has been to move onward and upward in the corporation, the advent of Stage #1 of that dream, relocation, with the complications of family reactions and the housing problem, comes as a shock.
2. The employee needs to know the exact nature of the new job, the financial ramifications and something about the location he is being transferred to.
3. The employee needs *time* to put it all together in his head.

GOOD TIMING HELPS

Schedule the first discussions of a transfer for a morning hour—9:00 or 10:00 A.M. There is a sound psychological reason for this. An employee is better able to accept, understand and begin to deal with this possibly threatening idea in the morning when he is fresh, rather than late in the day. It also gives him the rest of the day to think about it in the supportive atmosphere of work and possibly discuss it with some of his colleagues. If it involves a raise and promotion, you can be fairly sure many colleagues will either congratulate him or be openly envious, which is bound to make him think positively about the move.

If he's presented with the news at the end of the day, he's faced with the immediate necessity of informing his family before he has had a chance to think it through himself. Informing the family is often difficult. Give the guy a head start.

BE SERIOUS

In business, it's customary to joke about important matters. The gain or loss of a big account; the rise or fall of an executive so remote that no one you know has even met him—this is the small change of company humor.

Some managers use company humor to sell relocation, "Jack, old buddy, you've finally hit the jackpot! You're being sent to San Francisco. I'm not kidding! Of course, it means a big fat raise for you, but you've got to watch out for Charlie Simmons—he'll cut your throat if he can."

Don't be surprised if Jack doesn't laugh. It's his raise and his promotion. It's his throat, too.

THE BETTER WAY

Even though you and Jack are best buddies, for this kind of announcement you have to put on your managerial hat. Start out something like this: "Look Jack, you may not want this, but the company thinks and I *know* you're really doing a ter-terific job. There's this great opening in San Francisco and you're the obvious choice. So how about it?"

The same approach is appropriate if you never saw Jack before in your life. Except that you rewrite the script.

This time it goes: "Mr. Jacobs, you have an excellent record with the company. In fact, your performance has been outstanding. Everyone agrees. Now something has come up. There's an opening in our San Francisco office that we feel you're the right person to fill. Of course, it means a raise and promotion, but it also means you would have to move to San Francisco, which you may or may not want to do.

"We're prepared to help you in any way we can with the move. Don't give me your answer now, take a little time to think it over. But let me fill you in now on most of the details."

BE PREPARED

Be prepared with the facts about the job. Describe to him the exact nature of the work, how it differs from his present job, the salary increase (if there is one). If there isn't, you'll want to mention the potential for future increases; his place in the company family hierarchy; the numbers and kinds of people he'll be working for or with; and who will be working for him.

Throughout, emphasize the advantages of the job for Jack, and the advantages to the company of having Jack in that particular spot.

Be prepared to do most of the talking at this point. The first announcement of a transfer is a lot for anyone to absorb. If you ramble on about the details of the job, this gives him a chance to catch his breath. He probably can't absorb and won't remember much of what you're saying. At this point, his mind is dealing with the gross fact of transfer; many details will not sink in. On the other hand, some of the most trivial (to you) may.

A promising salesman once quit after a transfer because, as he put it, "*They* told me I'd have my own secretary. Now I find I have to share one."

Don't be tempted to embellish the job description. Be prepared to answer questions about the job and the company's policy about relocation costs. If you don't know, don't invent! Say, "I don't know, but I'll find out." And follow through on the promise.

Do be prepared with the facts about Jack. If you're his immediate superivisor or otherwise in a position to know his work firsthand, there's no problem. But if it's a large company and you're the manager assigned to inform Jack of the transfer, do your homework. Don't rely on hearsay.

"Ever since you came here right out of college to work in the mail room we've had our eye on you," sounds wonderful. It may not sound wonderful to Jack if in fact he was hired right out of high school to work in the shipping department.

"You really racked up a great record in the Minneapolis office." Nothing wrong with that—unless it was the Chicago office.

Are there managers who do this? Yes.

TAKE IT EASY

Different people react differently to the news of transfer. If an employee is visibly distressed, end the interview quickly, suggest he take some time to think about it and set up another appointment to discuss it further.

On the other hand, if the employee accepts before you've had a chance to go into detail, remember the words of the movie mogul who told his staff, "Don't say 'yes' till I finish talking!"

With the overeager beaver, you may be forced to play father figure, pointing out to him that there's more to a move than just a raise. He has to think realistically of what the move will mean to his family emotionally; what it'll mean in terms of the cost of living—in short, all the things *his wife is going to bring up*. Get there first!

Beware of Mr. Cool. Be wary of the cool customer who accepts the news without so much as a flicker of an eyelid. It's more than a little unusual for a live person to absorb the news of a major life change with no show of emotion whatsoever.

He may have all sorts of hidden fears and resentments and mask them to save face. Try to break the ice and draw him out. Diplomatically! Don't interrogate like a district attorney! Establish a safe atmosphere by stressing the point that he is free to turn down the move if he wants to. Do point out that relocation is by its very nature quite literally unsettling. Suggest strongly and warmly that he consult with his wife and family and consider the full economic implications of the move before making any final decision.

Whatever an employee's reaction, by all means discourage him or her from making any final decisions at this initial point. Wind up the interview by saying, "Well, I guess you've got a lot of things to think about and talk over with your family. Let's quit now and plan to meet again on . . ." Set a date then and there for the second discussion.

As the employee leaves your office, offer whatever printed material you have on your company's relocation policies. In fact, place it right in his hands. Don't let him leave without it.

THE SECOND INTERVIEW

At the second interview, an occasional transferee will show up with the economic facts of the transfer analyzed, family matters settled and ready to roll. This is rare. Very rare.

In the majority of cases he will come in full of doubts, conflicts and questions. Particularly questions.

Make it clear at the beginning of the discussion that no decision need be made at this time; that you realize the decision to move is a difficult one; that you want him to feel free to discuss any aspect of the move that is a problem.

Keep the door open for the employee to express negative as well as positive feelings. This is very important! If you stress that internal conflict is a normal by-product of a transfer situation, the transferee will tend to settle down and relax about the whole business.

DON'T LISTEN TO THE WORDS, LISTEN TO THE MUSIC

Efficient listening in a relocation situation works to the advantage of both parties. It enables the transferee simultaneously to get all his concerns off his chest and also to organize his own thoughts—just through talking it all through with an impartial listener. As any priest or psychiatrist will tell you, a person can often, if not always, find the answer to a complex question himself, merely by going through the *process* of relating it all step-by-step to a sympathetic listener. The confusing components of the puzzle fall into place through educated listening ("listening with the third ear," is what psychiatrist Theodore Reik called it) and that helps you do your job better. Letting the employee pour out his half-formed thoughts on every aspect of the move (with a minimum of interruption from you!) gives you a grasp of what's really bothering him.

So don't listen just to the words; listen to the music. If the emphasis seems to be on family problems, that's the topic to pursue, but try to figure out if there is more to the story than he lets on. If the talk is all of money, its time to bone up on the financial fine points of the move, but listen to hear if something seems to be going unsaid.

The second interview, if conducted properly, doesn't necessarily produce the answer. But it does, if handled properly, at least define the question.

WHAT IF HE SAYS NO?

Some employees refuse relocation on the second interview. Don't show surprise or anger. Don't in any way criticize or attempt to argue with him.

Instead, nod your head thoughtfully and say something like, "I see. Well, I'm sorry you feel this way, but are you sure you've given it enough thought? We really need you in the new spot, and there are a lot of advantages to you that you may not have thought of. Why not think about it some more? There's still plenty of time to think about it and discuss it."

Ask him to elaborate on his main objections to the move.

After acknowledging that his concerns are understood (remember they're real for him even if they seem silly to you) offer alternative views, if you can; in a pleasant way, bring out the other side of the story. If it's family problems, draw him out on them (gently!) and suggest there may be ways the company can help. If there are financial problems, offer to develop new information that may affect his decision.

But at this point, don't take no for an answer. Or yes for an answer either. (A man convinced against his will is of the same opinion still.) Wind up the discussion and set up a date for meeting again. Be prepared in your own mind that you may still get a no-go answer. But take comfort in the fact that you gave it your best shot.

AT EVERY INTERVIEW: BE ALERT TO HIDDEN PROBLEMS

If you sense during an interview that an employee is not leveling with you, try even harder to establish trust and confidence. A very personal problem may be a hidden handicap.

A design engineer who really wanted the transfer job offer kept giving excuses for turning it down. His children were in school. But, said the manager, there are even better schools in the new location than there are in the old. The engineer went on to spell out with less and less conviction that his wife had a job (as a part-time saleswoman); that he'd gotten sort of used to Harrisburg; and that he really didn't care about promotion anyway.

This from a man who had just gotten two raises and was considered a company star!

Finally the truth came out. The designer finally admitted to his supervisor, under a strict pledge of secrecy, that he had a sister confined to a mental hospital. This was a source of great embarrassment to his family; his mother and brothers considered the sister a disgrace and ignored the fact of her existence. At this point, he was her only visitor. He believed, for reasons known only to himself but understandable to most of us, that this news would be as shocking to his supervisors as it was to his seventy-nine-year-old mother.

It wasn't. His manager referred him to the company nurse who along with the medical consultant to the corporation quickly and quietly found a comparable institution a short driving distance away from the new location.

BE PATIENT

Don't show irritation if the employee asks a question that you answered in the first interview. Remember: the transferee has a lot of information to deal with in a relatively short time, and under stress, attention and retention spans are shortened.

> JACK JACOBS: What exactly am I supposed to *do* in the Chicago office?
>
> THE WRONG WAY: Well I really don't know what the job entails except that you'll be department head. I explained all that on Monday.
>
> THE RIGHT WAY: Well, you'll still be designing of course, except that you'll have four guys under you. But that shouldn't be any problem for you. You know, you have real executive ability. We've noticed that in the way you handle the younger men.

Or, consider the following situation.

> JACK JACOBS: What bothers my wife is that we'll have to go on a house hunting trip. We'll have to get sitters and she feels she'll need more than three days to find a house. We have never left the children before.
>
> THE WRONG WAY: You'll be reimbursed, and the cost of sitters is included. It's all in those booklets I gave you on Monday. What's the matter, didn't you bother to read them?

The Right Way: Leaving children for the first time is difficult. I remember when my wife and and I had to do it. We all have to get to that point sometimes. It might even turn out to be a nice thing for you, sort of like your first vacation away from the children. The company pays almost all expenses including baby-sitting. Here [pulling out a booklet on the company relocation policy], you see, it says we pay for . . .

Be prepared to make the same point over and over again in several different ways.

AND DON'T LOSE YOUR COOL

Some employees will voice their negative reactions to a move in tones of anger, sarcasm or both. Don't, no matter how you're tempted, respond in kind. For example:

Employee: The move to New York is great except that with mortgage rates what they are we'll probably have to pitch a tent along the East River.

Wrong: What do you want? A suite at the Waldorf? Your the tenth guy in two weeks with the same line.

Right: It's tough, I know. But it's the same for everybody who moves these days, and there's always a way around it. Our relocation people [or the real estate brokers favored by the company at the new location] are pretty sharp. I'm sure you'll find something that works for you when you go on your house hunting trip. You may be surprised at what you find in some of the suburban areas, particularly the smaller towns.

Or, the following situation might confront you.

> EMPLOYEE: Couldn't you have come up with something better Kansas City for me? Sherm Marshall says it's the pits.
>
> THE WRONG WAY: Sherm Marshall has problems that have nothing to do with Kansas City; he'd have them anywhere he lived.
>
> THE RIGHT WAY: Well, you know Sherm, he likes to complain. Why don't you talk to Pete Edwards or Mary Brown? I hear they're pretty happy with the setup there. Drop in on them when you go on your house hunting trip.

Important point: if the employee sounds doubtful about any aspect of the new location, be sure to remind him that he'll get a chance to evaluate it at first hand on preliminary visits.

THE THIRD INTERVIEW

By the third interview, the employee has usually made up his mind whether it's go or stay. He may, of course, have lingering doubts or leftover questions. This is the time to reexamine or answer them. If there are problems that *seriously* need further exploration, you can grant an extension. But generally speaking, the third meeting is put-up-or-shut-up time.

If you feel that every aspect of the relocation has been probed in detail and the employee is still indecisive, end the interview by saying "Okay, Jack [or Mr. Jacobs], I guess we've covered all the points as fully as we can cover them. I'll expect your final decision Monday morning."

No More Mr. Nice Guy

Don't get so carried away by being Mr. Nice Guy; don't, for instance, suggest further interviews. Some people will take advantage of such an offer and you could end up in the role of friendly job and/or marriage counselor to Jack Jacobs for the next few weeks, if not months. You aren't going to like that. Neither is the company.

If He Says Yes

Congratulations are in order. Also the reassurance that the help provided is just the beginning, that if problems develop in connection with the move, the company will continue to help, because the company and the employee are in this together.

If He Says No

Understanding is in order. If the discussions of the move have followed the above guidelines, you and he should both understand that he is turning down the move for good and legitimate reasons. Reassure him that this turndown will in no way effect his career with the company. If he was good enough to be offered transfer and promotion at this point, he'll still be good enough when his personal situation has changed. End on a positive note. You may not have achieved a desirable transfer; neither have you shattered the morale of a valuable employee.

THE GROUP MOVE

Not surprisingly, the group move, in which a whole division of perhaps 400 employees is transported bodily from one location to another, is the biggest headache for corporations and most threatening to employee morale. As well it might be.

Group moves are a relatively new phenomenon in industry, and most companies have a lot of problems coping with them just because they haven't had to handle such an exodus too often.

When a company is contemplating a group move or has almost completed plans for one, the conventional scheme is to keep the plans a dark secret from members of the group involved, lest they panic.

This never works. There are no dark secrets in corporations. Secretaries know, personnel and accounting department clerks know. It does no good to swear these employees to secrecy. Somebody always tells somebody (swearing *him* to secrecy) and—woosh!—the news is out.

Or at least the rumor is out. The affected department gets wind of a move on the office grapevine, inevitably, even before it's a sure thing. Promptly, misinformation explodes along the corridors and sometimes panic.

"Hey Joe, have you heard the latest? They're moving us to Texas."

"Oh sure, I heard about that, but it's just the guys in sales."

"No, *everybody*! The whole division!"

"You're kidding!"

"No, my sister-in-law works in J.D.'s office and she heard them talking about it."

"Oh great! It's not so bad for you, you're single, but I got four kids. Well, back to the unemployment line. Hey, Manny, you hear we're moving to Texas?"

"Sure! I heard that a month ago. But it isn't Texas, it's West Virginia. Besides it isn't supposed to happen for two, maybe three years."

"That's not what I heard, I heard next month."

"Oh God, I'm supposed to get *married* next month."

"Well, happy honeymoon in the Ozarks! I'll probably be getting divorced. One thing I know about Millie; she's not leaving Bayside."

Let's Shake Them Up!

All (or almost all) experienced managers could have written this scenario themselves. Or something resembling it. Old J. D. Harkness explains, "Oh sure, we knew they were bound to find out a move was in the wind. Well, let 'em, it shakes them up a little. They all go running around, scared they're going to lose their jobs, so when we tell them we're moving them, at our expense, they're grateful to go. Keep 'em in suspense—that's my motto!"

One result of the suspense—which lasted for five months—was a sharp drop in productivity and company morale. And by the time the move (to Albuquerque, New Mexico, as it turned out) was officially announced, a number of valuable employees had sought and found jobs elsewhere.

A substantial part of our own business is supervising group moves for big corporations. There's nothing mysterious about our technique. Yes, we're psychologists by training, but, no, we don't get large numbers of people to relocate by brainwashing, mass hypnosis or other arcane methods unavailable to businessmen.

There's nothing we do that any company can't do for itself—*if* it gets its act together. It's a matter of organization, information properly channelled, plus a large dose of human understanding. And an even large dose of just plain common sense.

Here's the way we do it.

As soon as the decision to move the group is final, letters (not memos) are sent out to all hands *at their homes,* announcing the move and inviting employees *and their wives* to attend a briefing session and presentation at either company headquarters or a hotel. Example:

Dear Mr. and Mrs. Kinney:

The management of Harkness Corporation is very happy to announce that we are expanding. We are establishing a new base in Tampa, Florida, and your division, the Bayside Division, has been selected to go there. Naturally, we hope everyone will understand the advantages to the company of relocating the division— to say nothing of the long-term advantages to individual employees. We also understand that relocating is a problem for many, but not a problem that can't be solved.

Therefore, I hope you'll be my guest at a morning coffee and presentation, Tuesday, April 15, at 11:00 A.M., in the Grand Ballroom of the Carlsbad Hotel, at 211 Gresham Boulevard, where we can all learn what this move will mean to us, as members of the Harkness family.

Cordially,

J. D. Harkness

Substitutions are allowed. Many companies have preferred to make it cocktails and dinner at the Carlsbad Hotel—that's a matter of company style and regional preference. Go by *what you think the wives would like.*

At the morning meeting, have coffee and danish at the ready on buffet tables with plenty of waiters hovering about to pour and have folding seats set up in the Grand Ballroom.

(Like a sales meeting, you know?) If it's an evening meeting, keep the cocktail hour brief, serve dinner about half an hour after the arrival time and be ready to roll with the presentation as the waiters are passing out coffee. Again, like a sales meeting. Essentially, of course, what this *is* a sales meeting.

The Presentation Goes Like This

We generally recommend that a company spokesman start by explaining the company's reasons for the move and acknowledging up front that this may present a problem for the individuals involved, but also has many positive aspects. The purpose of the meeting is to provide all the facts about the upcoming move and to give the employees an opportunity to raise their questions.

A good slide presentation of the new location, showing the cultural assets, historic landmarks or other attractive features of the area is always appreciated. The slides should be something of a travelogue, so the employees can see their new hometown for themselves. There should also be pictures of houses in all price ranges that have sold within the last three months, along with the selling prices.

Talk frankly about current real estate values and explain carefully to the audience the kind of help they can expect from their company in making this move. Some representative from the new community or from a consulting group there can brief your audience about the advantages of the new location: schooling, medical services and other particular advantages.

It's a good idea to distribute "Survival Kits" to everyone—packages of printed material reiterating what your people have been told and shown, including photographs of the new location, a good map, the details of the company relocation policy, plus booklets and brochures from the chamber of commerce, local historical societies or other civic minded groups in the new location.

Don't forget: your company is going to be pumping tax dollars into the town or city you have chosen to move to, so the city fathers and public services should be counted on to help make your move successful. The board of education will almost always be delighted to prepare special material welcoming your employees and detailing the many advantages of its school system. The local hospital or medical center and no doubt the public library will do likewise.

A reproduction of a press clipping from the *Cartersville Courier*, headlined "Harkness Company Moving to Cartersville," isn't going to tell your employees much that they don't know already in the way of useful facts. But it's a great morale builder. Even if the local reporter has some facts slightly wrong, a news story fixes in the relocatee's mind a most welcome piece of news; he or she will be, if not a very important person, at least a pretty important person in Cartersville. And that's nice to know at a time of some uncertainty and transition.

When we consult for a corporation we give a brief talk on the corporation's concern for its employees' welfare and that of the employees' families. We explain all available programs to help people make their transfer decisions; help them with their personal issues in the relocation; and help them get their emotional assets moved along with their physical possessions.

At the end of the formal presentation, a company representative should invite questions from the audience. The questions are answered by management people if they concern company policy and sometimes by us if they touch on family-related problems.

The presentation is best ended by a company representative who reiterates the date of the move, encourages employees to study their "Survival Kits" and, if there are problems, to make appointments with their direct supervisors or otherwise designated management representatives to discuss them.

Any company can follow this pattern and modify it to its own needs.

SPECIAL FOR SMALL COMPANIES

Thousands of small companies relocate a few employees each year. These companies cannot afford to use the same relocation management services deployed by the giant corporations, but they can compensate by adding the personal touch. The same principles of manager-employee talks apply whether you're a giant, mid-sized or small corporation.

Take a very small company moving all its operations. It's a small circulation specialized sports magazine called *Fly Fisherman*. *Fly Fisherman* has traditionally had its offices in New York because New York has been for many years, the publishing capital. It's a very profitable magazine—or has been. In the past, editorial and production costs have been low and advertising revenue substantial. After all, where else can the manufacturers of rods and lures find a ready-made audience? But all that has changed. Paper has gone up, and printing has gone up, rents have gone sky-high.

And so, *Fly Fisherman* is moving to New Hampshire. Paper costs are the same, but printing is cheaper and rent is certainly lower. Writers? Its writers are located all over the country; they can mail their articles to New Hampshire as easily as to New York.

Ed Cameron, the publisher, having made this decision, was afraid to tell his key employees. First, he was afraid he would lose them if he moved the magazine out of New York and he'd feel guilty about depriving them of jobs. And so he simply put off announcing the move.

He confided his problem to his neighbor, an executive with one of our client companies, and the neighbor suggested he talk to us.

We advised Ed not to back off from the problem but to be totally honest with the employees, telling them the economic reasons the move was necessary and simultaneously how valuable they were to the operation. We also gave him a list of benefits and services that other companies provide for relocating employees. We suggested he use the list as a guideline. We did stress, however, that since his company was not in a position to guarantee a low mortgage rate like giant corporations the key to a successful move for him was how he presented the move and that his attitude toward his employees had to make his concern very clear.

The key man in the operation was the editor, Marty Timmons.

Ed and his wife, Alice, invited Marty and his wife, Mimi, to dinner at the best expense account restaurant in New York. Well, anyway, one of the best. Ed laid it straight on the line: what the company's business problems were; why the move was necessary; and how much he hoped that Marty and Mimi could see their way clear to go along. He told them that the magazine would pay for moving expenses and a house hunting trip and that in the small New Hampshire town he had selected affordable housing should be no problem.

Marty and Mimi were just as honest. Fishing and outdoor sports were Marty's life and Mimi's hobby. *Fly Fisherman* was having its difficulties paying its rent in Manhattan, but Marty and Mimi were having even more.

"Especially on the salary you pay me," said Marty.

"Expect a raise," said Ed.

What About the Children?

"Kids? Don't be silly," said Mimi. "I'm scared to send them to public school in New York and I can't afford private school. I'm for the village schoolhouse in New Hampshire."

The other key editorial worker was art director Lou Kline, and Ed repeated the dinner with Lou, his wife, Kathy, and another very important lady, Miss Betsy Perkins, aged fifty plus, production manager and perfectionist, without whom, everyone agreed, *Fly Fisherman* could not function.

"Leave *Fly Fisherman*?" Lou said, puzzled that the publisher should have thought it possible. "You don't understand. Look, I could make more money as an art director for an advertising agency. But in case you have forgotten, I—we, that is—have won two important design awards from journalism schools. At *Fly Fisherman*, I don't get paid a lot . . ."

"Expect a raise," said Ed automatically.

"Right," said Lou. "But as I was saying, at our magazine, I can produce something I'm proud of and get recognition for. And that's important."

"Could you take New Hampshire?"

"Could I?" said Lou. "Kathy and I have been trying desperately to figure out how we can eventually have a place in the country. Where I can paint and she can grow vegetables. And here it is, complete with job."

And Miss Betsy? "I thought you'd never ask," she said, "but if you want *my* opinion, an outdoor life magazine *belongs* in New England not in New York City. I came from there, more years ago than I care to admit and I'm ready to go back. Of course, I expect a raise. In fact, a substantial one."

Often, employees who elect to go with small businesses do so because they believe in that business. Whether it's a magazine or a small manufacturer.

Anything less than the honest and open way in which Ed informed his people would have disrupted this confidence. As it turned out, most of the staff has moved to New Hampshire and *Fly Fisherman* is a going concern in its outdoor-conscious setting.

MANAGERS ARE PEOPLE, TOO

In going over the first pages of this chapter, we can hear the reaction of many managers.

It boils down to: "It's all very well for those guys to sound off about what the ideal manager should do. But in *my* company . . ."

Enough already. We know, we know.

This book has been and is concerned primarily with the problems of the potential transferee and his family. But there is certainly another side of it. The manager's side of it.

The task of informing the transferee in an individual or group move often falls on the heads of managers whose jobs have nothing to do with relocation.

Bill Baxter, for example, told us, "I'm supposed to keep my department running, meet my quotas, and now work overtime as Dear Abby for transferees who don't want to go. I can't hack it."

Right. Every manager is concerned about those under him and wants things to go well for them and the company. But all too often the middle manager is caught in the squeeze. If he's a good manager (*especially* if he's a good manager), he takes the ultimate responsibility for the transfer and the people in his division.

Which means that he is, theoretically at least, required to be familiar with financing at the level of a tax accountant, the real estate market at the level of a national brokerage firm, family problems at the level of a marriage counselor and the new town or city at the level of its chamber of commerce.

He usually isn't. In fact, sometimes he isn't even familiar with the relocation policy of his own company, especially if none exists in concrete form.

TOOLING UP FOR RELOCATION

The harrassed Bills of the corporate world can take heart. Somebody is listening. Quite probably, your own company.

Almost every corporation with any volume of relocation is looking hard at the way transfers are handled within the company. Industry is beginning to realize that the economics and human factors in transfers make them a task that cannot be handled by individual managers as an extra duty.

The answer to one part of the problem, housing, is pretty well solved. Over 75 percent of companies that move a lot of employees use relocation management firms to handle the practicalities of the move (see appendix). These companies operate in different ways. All provide transferring employees a look at a choice of appropriate quarters in the new location and local brokers to show the house hunters around. Some companies also buy at a fair market price the old house and sell a new home to the transferee at a fair market price.

But even the most efficient relocation company can't perform at optimum efficiency if it is dealing at random with all kinds of people within the employing corporation.

What's the next step? Setting up, as many companies are doing, a relocation department headed by a relocation manager. The relocation manager is on a level with general managers and reports directly to executive management. He has his own staff.

The department acts as central clearing house for all information dealing with relocation. On file in printed form (and available to all) are brochures and pamphlets spelling out the company's relocation policy, benefits available, pertinent tax information and practical advice on moving. (These lists can be obtained from the Department of Internal Revenue, the Department of Interstate Commerce, various van lines or quite possibly your own relocation company. Or for that matter, the last chapter of this book.)

The department is responsible for supervising group moves. In the case of individual transfers, although the individual may be notified of transfer by the relocation department, discussions of the move are usually between the transferee and his immediate supervisor. Both should be supplied with background information as a basis for discussion. Ultimately, the way news of transfer is communicated to the employee will have an impact on his decision to move or not to move, and in the long run on the way he views the company.

Even though the relocation director is designated as the

person to whom employees should direct questions, doubts and concerns about moving, they tend to go to their own supervisors. Even though the relocation director is designated to communicate company philosophy and policy on relocation, in practice, the attitude of the general manager of the division is likely to prevail. In a large corporation, the attitudes of general managers vary considerably, so employees and supervisors get different messages.

The executive board of the company had best define its relocation policy and philosophy very concretely and communicate it to the relocation director. His is not simply a job of conveying information to division managers. It's making sure they understand it. And to communicate a progressive relocation policy, general managers must have an understanding of the psychological needs of employees and their families. Our client companies have found our training seminars for managers useful to achieve this end.

An effective relocation department can solve the practical problems of relocation or at least go a long way toward smoothing them, but managers must realize that it's not only household goods that need to be moved. The relocating family must move their emotions too.

HEART IS THE HEART OF THE MATTER

If industry is to commit itself to relocation as a way of life, it must be alert to the wide range of emotional problems. Many companies now are aware of this, but are struggling with simultaneous feelings of wanting to help but being afraid to suggest that their employees need help and afraid that in offering help they will violate the employees' private worlds.

We must begin to acknowledge that all aspects of human needs and functioning come into play in a relocation. When the psychological dimension comes up, don't fall back on clichés or jokes about shrinks, or make it seem that abnormal behavior is the topic. Relocation is a naturally stress-producing situation. Almost all normal people are, one way or another, upset by it. But it can be dealt with humanely and with financial prudence.

This philosophy must originate at the top management level. The buck starts there.

THE NUTS AND BOLTS OF MOVING

The trauma of moving can be soothed if you arrange to have the details of the physical move run smoothly. Herewith, practical tips for getting your belongings from one house to another.

THE TIME TO MOVE

You may have no control over your timing, but if it's at all possible, try to avoid moving in summer. Yours are not the only children who will balk at having to move in the middle of a school year, so you'll find that moving companies are super busy during summer vacations. There's more chance of things going wrong in the summer: dates not being kept; boxes being delivered to someone else's house; heartbreaking breakage; and all the other notorious headaches.

If you must move between June and September, at least try to schedule your move for the middle of the month. Though it may mean paying double rent for a month, it could prove to be a wise investment in the long run not to have the movers working for you during their most overworked peak times.

CHOOSING A MOVING FIRM

Your company or relocation company may choose a mover for you. But whether the designated van line is their choice or yours, here's how to proceed.

The earlier you begin the better. Though the assignment of a specific van may not be made until a few days before your move, it's wise to give a moving company from four to six weeks advance notice whenever possible. The more lead time you can allow, the more likely it is that you'll get to move on your preferred date. Even with sufficient advance notice, most firms will request alternate delivery dates.

If you're selecting the moving company, it's a good idea to shop around. Inquire about the different services offered by different companies. (Will you need to store some of your furniture until your new house is ready? Does your mover arrange for this storage or is it left up to you?)

Then, watch to see how carefully the mover inspects your belongings before giving you an estimate. While it's *your* obligation to point out *exactly* what is to be moved—and we do mean exactly—a reputable mover will be sure to ask questions. And probably quite a few questions.

An estimate should not be the sole basis of choosing a mover, though. Estimates are no more than estimates, after all. (See below.) Also keep in mind whether the firm has an office near your final destination (a fact that will assume great importance if something does happen to go wrong). And *do* ask your friends or business associates who have moved recently if they were happy with the firm they chose. That should probably be the key factor in influencing your final choice.

ALWAYS GET AN ESTIMATE

And get it in writing and keep the paper in a very accessible place. While an estimate is not a binding contract or a guarantee of a future price, it does tell you what the approximate cost of your move should be. If one estimate is substantially below others, be suspicious and ask *lots* of questions. The extra low estimate may mean extra weak packing boxes for your favorite china.

The estimate is very importnat, too, because movers (as you probably know), accept only cash, money orders, certified checks or travelers checks as payment, and your burly friends must be paid *before* your belongings are unloaded at their final destination. If your final bill exceeds the estimate by more than 10 percent, federal regulations give you the explicit right to pay only the estimated charges plus 10 percent upon delivery, with the balance due within fifteen working days.

HOW MUCH WILL YOUR MOVE COST?

The exact cost of your move cannot be determined until your shipment has been loaded on the van and weighed. Under tariff regulations established by the Interstate Commerce Commission, the transportation charge is based on the actual weight of your goods (this is why it's important to show *everything* to the estimator) and the distance traveled.

The easiest way to move is to have the moving company do all the packing, but this is also the most expensive way. Packing charges are based on the size and number of cartons used, with an extra charge if you want the mover to do any unpacking at the destination.

WHO IS LIABLE?

Protecting your household goods during a move is important. If you choose to pack your belongings yourself, the mover is not liable for breakage (for more about packing yourself, see below), although some damage coverage is still included.

The mover's liability depends on the valuation statement on the bill of lading (the receipt for your goods that will be given to you when they are picked up). However, you should give some thought beforehand to how much protection you want.

As part of the basic moving charge, you receive minimum protection of 60 cents per pound for each article lost or damaged. You can also choose to upgrade the rate of coverage to $1.25 per pound; or to declare the total value of your goods and pay an additional charge of 50 cents per each $100 of higher protection. The amount of protection you want should be noted on the bill of lading before it is signed.

If you are moving pieces of fine art or valuable antiques, arrange beforehand with your insurance broker for specific coverage to protect these items while you move. Check your homeowner's policy; it may include coverage of your possessions in transit. While you're making these arrangements, ask your broker to arrange the transfer of all personal property insurance to your new address as of the date of your move. If you're being transferred, check with your company to see if they provide blanket moving insurance.

PREPARING TO MOVE

As soon as you find out that you're going to be moving, begin sorting through everything you own—deciding what to take with you and discarding whatever you *still* haven't found a use for since the last time you moved. This is an ideal time for relatively painless housecleaning. Whatever you can part with won't have to be packed, shipped and unpacked at some expense—and won't haunt you again during your next move!

Tackle a few drawers or a closet each day. Contact your favorite local charity to arrange for donations of furniture, kitchen gadgets, books or clothing. Ask if they can arrange to have these items picked up or if you must transport them to a central location. If you get a receipt from the charity, you may be eligible for a sizable income tax reduction. Or, if you prefer, consider holding a garage sale.

WHAT THE MOVERS WILL NOT TAKE

You have to provide for things that moving companies cannot take in their vans. Plants are one. Arrange to give them away to close neighbors as farewell gifts or plan on taking them along in your car. (Do remember that certain states have restrictions on the transfer of plants across their borders, including quarantine regulations, etc. Check beforehand with the authorities in states you will be passing through.)

Pets are usually transported along with the family; they may also be shipped by air or rail express.

Talk to your bank about moving valuables, jewelry and important documents. Many banks can arrange the transfer of the contents of your safe deposit box for you. Or you can elect to send valuables by insured, registered mail. If you do transport valuables with you, check with your insurance broker to be sure you have adequate protection against their loss or theft enroute. Since it is nearly impossible to insure cash, you might consider carrying traveler's checks for large amounts of money.

Movers *will* take furs on the van, although many people prefer to transport them personally. Either way, be sure you have adequate insurance protection.

A MONTH OR TWO BEFORE THE MOVE

Arrange to have major cleaning jobs done: rugs, draperies, furniture, etc. Deal with people whose work you've already found satisfactory and you'll have the pleasure of arriving in your new home with clean, fresh possessions.

Begin to compile a list of people and businesses that will have to be notified of your change of address. Get the forms from your local post office and fill out a few each day. Do magazines and journals first; they usually prefer two months notice whenever possible. Here's a list of most of the other people and places you'll need to notify:

> post office
> utilities (gas, electric, water, telephone)
> doctors and dentists (arrange to have medical records transferred and ask if they can recommend physicians in your new location)
> lawyers and accountants
> schools
> banks
> drugstore (obtain copies of your family's current prescriptions)
> optometrist
> department stores (transfer or close out accounts)
> clubs
> the library
> city hall (garbage collection)
> the motor vehicle bureau (change registration and license)

Also begin to notify friends and business associates of your expected move.

NOW IT'S FOUR WEEKS TO MOVING DAY

It may seem obvious: this is the time to start using up frozen foods, pantry shelf canned goods and household supplies. Buy groceries in small quantities from now on; they're heavy and more expensive to move than they are to buy new.

Consider packing up books that you'll not need right away and mailing them at the special fourth class book rate. It will be cheaper than letting the mover take them.

NOW IT'S TWO TO THREE WEEKS BEFORE THE MOVE

If you're planning to drive to your new home, have your car checked to be sure it's in top condition for the trip. Check tires, brakes and windshield wipers. Have the car lubricated, oil and oil filter changed if necessary. Also be sure that the points, spark plugs and other parts of the ignition system are in first-rate condition and that you have a complete tool kit to take with you for emergency use.

This is the time to make your final travel plans, including hotel or motel reservations en route to your new home if you'll need them.

Prepare a floor plan of your new home to help in unloading, unpacking and furniture placement, especially for the heavy stuff.

Apply a light layer of paste wax to your furniture to guard against potential scratching and protect the finish against accidental water contact.

If you will be moving any appliances, set a date with a reliable service firm to prepare them for shipment (preferably the day before your move). Depending on the appliance, pre-moving as well as post-moving service may be needed. Check the owner's manual of your refrigerator, freezer, range, washer or dryer for instructions.

TWO OR THREE DAYS BEFORE THE MOVE

Empty the refrigerator and freezer so they can dry out for at least twenty-four hours before the movers arrive (leave the doors open for a day if you can). If the insides are not completely dry, mold and mildew may develop.

Check the contents of your bureau drawers, removing all valuables and breakable items. Blouses, blankets, sweaters, etc., can all be left in the drawers; heavy linens should not be. If you're moving clothing in a wardrobe, pin items to the hangers, so that vibrations or bumps will not cause them to fall off.

Remove drapes, curtains, shades, blinds and traverse rods from the windows if you can. Otherwise the movers will charge you extra for this service.

Dispose of all flammable items such as cleaning fluids, gasoline and other chemicals; the moving company cannot transport these items.

THE DAY BEFORE THE MOVE

This is the day to make up a box of essentials you'll need immediately on arrival: bedroom linens and bathroom towels, soap, toilet tissue, paper cups, light bulbs, snack food, instant coffee makings. Label the box "For Immediate Use" and instruct the movers to put it on the van last, so that it gets unloaded first.

If the moving company will be doing your packing, chances are this will be the day. Be on hand to supervise. Advise the packers firmly of all fragile items that need special treatment and identitfy items that should *not* be moved. *Don't* ever be intimidated by the movers! If they're not doing it *your* way, speak up. If necessary, speak up again or call their boss at his office. Remember, you're the boss!

Of course, you've decided what the children will do on

moving day—perhaps they could spend the morning with neighbors. Whatever you decide, be sure to keep them out of the way of the moving men.

MOVING DAY

You'll be putting in a long, hard day and you'll want to have a clear head for it. Be sure every member of the family has a good substantial breakfast. Make sure everybody knows who is to do what and where and why. If you live on a busy street, you'll want a trusted person to be near the open van at all times. Plan to be on hand from the minute the mover arrives until the last box is put on the van—and anticipate that the mover will be late. The Interstate Commerce Commission does require, however, that the mover adhere to the scheduled pickup and delivery dates. If there is an unforeseen delay, you should receive a new date well in advance.

Stay close to the van operator as he inspects and numbers your belongings. It is your responsibility to see that everything is properly described on the final inventory sheet. A well taken inventory should describe the condition of every piece of furniture and it should list every item put on the van.

When everything has been loaded, you'll want to read and recheck the inventory before signing it—and be certain to get a copy. At the same time you'll be asked to approve and sign a combination bill of lading and freight bill. This gives the terms and conditions of the move and serves as the official receipt for your goods. Make sure that the place of delivery and the declared valuation of your goods are shown correctly. When you have checked over the bill of lading completely and found everything in order, sign it and obtain your copy.

Although it may sound silly, check *again* that the mover has the correct delivery address—and, if possible, that he has a phone number where you can be reached.

Before locking up the house, check to see that the light

switches are off, the telephone has been disconnected, the furnace is turned down (but not off in winter) and the keys have been turned over to the new owners or tenants.

AT LAST: YOU'VE ARRIVED!

Remember: nothing will be unloaded until payment has been made.

The mover will place furniture as you direct. His men will lay rugs and set up beds, but they are not permitted to perform such specialty tasks as installing appliances, fixtures, curtain rods, etc.

As your belongings are unloaded from the van, check each item and note any change in condition on the inventory sheet. Also note anything that might be missing. The driver must also note these items on his inventory and give you a signed copy. Insist on this.

If you need to file a claim for loss or damage, do so as soon as possible with the carrier's office. Reputable moving companies will make prompt and equitable settlements, another reason for having carefully chosen your mover in the first place.

Here's wishing you a reasonably trouble free move. Remember: the nerves you expend are your own!

SPECIAL FOR SINGLES (DIVORCED AND OTHERWISE)

It's a common assumption that for single people relocation presents little problem. Supposedly, the worldly bachelor or the self-sufficient businesswoman can pack up and move at a moment's notice whenever the company calls. There's not even supposed to be the problem of selling the old house; since most single people tend to live in rental apartments, all problems are minor, right?

That's what married people think. Single people know differently, especially single women.

We've devoted most of this book so far to family people because families make up, statistically, the great majority of transferees. But that's changing. According to the latest census figures, young people are marrying later. The number of never married women has doubled between 1960 and 1979. It's no news that the divorce rate is up, way up, and divorced people are, for practical purposes, single. And in addition, some 1.3 million Americans of all ages are living together; they may think of themselves as couples even though corporations don't.

The single transferee obviously isn't concerned about a

wife's or husband's job or the children's schooling. Nonetheless, the single person has plenty of concerns, pressing concerns. They're neither more nor less traumatic, just different.

BREAKING AWAY

Single transferees in their early twenties are often leaving home for the first time. Some unmarried young people do move away from their families and set up housekeeping with roommates, but the majority live, if only for economic reasons, with their parents.

This is becoming more and more fashionable as our economy drives apartment rentals far beyond the financial ability of most young people starting to work.

First, there are the practical issues in setting up an apartment, and also the problems of learning to live alone, separate from friends, and finding a new network of support figures. Essentially everything that confronts the married couple is relevant.

The second trauma, which for some can be worse than the first, is the emotional separation from parents. Any insightful couple can remember some separation difficulties when they got married, even if they only moved a short distance away. Separation from parents at marriage is eased because you have the support of a loved one and a ready-made attachment to develop.

This doesn't apply to most young single people facing a transfer. It's not immature, sissy-like or disturbed to experience separation trauma. In fact, it's usually expected to some degree in most healthy functioning young people. Naturally, some are too deeply involved with parents, but that's rare and not of major concern.

Don't think that eagerness to get away from parents in the late teens (and up) means you're immune to the separation experience we are talking about. The feeling of wanting to "get out" is also normal, but this definitely doesn't exclude separation anxiety.

For those still living with parents at the time of the first transfer, breaking away can mean plenty of trauma, especially the practical difficulties of living alone (and it's just as hard for a young woman on a beginner's salary to feed herself decently and make her apartment livable as it is for a young man).

Homesick

Larry Borst is a case in point. Larry, aged twenty-five, had a well paying job as a lab technician in New Jersey. He is good-looking, self-assured and had plenty of dates and money to spend on them since he saved on rent by living with his parents. If you can picture the Fonz with an M.S. in chemistry, that was Larry.

When his company transferred him to the middle west, Larry was up, up and away. He packed his bags, kissed his mom goodbye, promised to write and zoomed off to new adventures. He had been seeking a way to move out of his parents' home for years; the transfer finally offered the financial resources and the perfect opportunity for the emotional break. If someone had suggested he was going to get homesick he would have thought him crazy and probably would have said so. Six months later he came to us, a very discouraged young man.

"I'm thinking of quitting this job and going home," he said.

"Why?" we asked. "Something wrong with the job?"

"The job is great," he said, "but that's about all. I'm living in a crummy, furnished apartment—well, truthfully, the apartment isn't so bad, but it's a mess all the time because who has time to clean it? I hired a cleaning woman but she quit on me because I asked her to wash my shirts the way my mom always did. I really thought living alone was going to be a ball, without my parents asking where I'm going, who with and what time I would be home. But, boy, I'm not finding it much fun.

"Then meals. Would you believe that's a problem? I know how to make coffee and my breakfast, but it's just too much of a pain in the morning, so I get a danish at the office from the coffee wagon and eat lunch in the company cafeteria. But then there's dinner. I always figured there'd be plenty of girls who would invite me to their houses for dinner. It hasn't been so easy to meet girls, and the three I have met don't know how to cook either. Most of the time they want to go to a restaurant and that gets pretty expensive.

"I visited my family over Christmas and it was really great. My old room—just the way I left it. Mom's cooking, seeing all my old friends, going to parties. In some ways I felt like a big baby. I really am confused. I couldn't get my old job back, I know, but I could get another. I think I'll chuck the whole thing and go home."

What Really Went Wrong For Larry?

Larry had vicariously lived the life of a young (TV style) bachelor, with girls galore and a penthouse style apartment, while actually living with his parents. His dream was quite far from the reality of a three room apartment, a not so easy time finding girlfriends and having to cope with cooking, cleaning and shopping—all the parts of bachelor living that Hollywood and TV leave out and that consequently get left out of daydreams.

This discrepancy between hope and reality was compounded by the total lack of preparation Larry had for what the separation experience would be like. Larry left with no notion that he would miss his parents or go through any kind of homesickness.

The most important element in coping with a trauma is to

be prepared for it, to have it explained beforehand so you know what to expect. If Larry had been prepared he would have avoided the most destructive part of this experience, namely, "In some ways I felt like a big baby. I really am confused." Lack of preparation led Larry to feel that there was something wrong with him and that he was immature. When you attempt to cope under stress, there is nothing more disruptive than berating yourself, discounting your feelings or calling them abnormal.

So—Be Prepared

Getting homesick is to be expected. Adjusting to living alone for the first time is rough. Getting depressed and wanting to go back home is not immature. It's entirely normal. There is usually a lot of work to living alone and there is rarely a lineup of heterosexual relationships just waiting for you to chose from.

So what Larrry went through is a normal experience and does not mean he is immature or a momma's boy. Acknowledge your feelings to someone, talk about them and realize that working them through will be a necessary growth experience for you.

DADDY'S GIRL

Grace Makharis is Larry's age and has a job very like Larry's, but when the company asked her to move, Grace flatly refused to go. "I know it's important to my career," she said. "I know I probably can't get as good a job here. But I can't move because of Papa."

Grace was, it developed, the youngest of three children. The two oldest had married and moved away. Grace lived with her widowed father, the proprietor of a hardware store.

"Is he an invalid?" we asked.

"Papa?" said Grace, "he certainly isn't. He's fifty-eight years old and healthy as a horse. He goes bowling twice a week. He's got more energy than I have!"

"You mean he just wants you for his housekeeper?"

"Oh, no," said Grace, "we have a housekeeper. Old Mrs. Kravitz, who lives down the block. She does the cleaning and some of the cooking. Mostly we take turns cooking. When it comes right down to it, Papa cooks better than I do. And there's no money problem. Papa's store does *very well.*"

"Then why?" we asked.

Grace sighed, "You just don't understand," she said. "My brother Tony is a man. My sister Elena is married and has children. I'm the single daughter! As Papa says, when the mother dies, it's the single daughter's job to take care of the father. He needs me!"

"As a wife?" we asked.

Grace was horrified. "You don't think . . ." she said.

No, of course we didn't think. But we did explain to Grace that her father's attitude was typical of many old-world ways. They are remnants of a rural culture in which "leftover" women (meaning those who didn't marry) were the responsibility (and still the property) of their male progenitors. It was all but a silent contractual obligation for these women to stay home and take over their mothers' jobs when those mothers died.

Grace had never thought of it this way, but she started thinking, right away.

"If I am, as you say, my father's 'wife,' well, I'm twenty-four and he's fifty-eight. And if I stay with him, in twenty years I'll own a hardware store."

"Is that what you want?" we asked.

"I don't know," said Grace. "I have to think about it."

We didn't see Grace for another two months. When we did, she had the problem all worked out.

"I don't want to own a hardware store," she said. "I don't want to spend my life selling bathroom fixtures. And I had it out with Papa. It took a lot of nerve, but I did it. I love my father and he knows I love him. But I explained to him that my staying on with him and keeping him company was preventing him from making a new life for himself. In the old country, fifty-eight may be over the hill, but in this country Papa still has a whole new life ahead of him.

"It suddenly occurred to me that my sticking around and keeping house for Papa was preventing him from meeting people his own age. He was using me as a crutch, and he doesn't need a crutch."

Events proved that Grace made the right decision. Over her father's protests, she moved to her job's new location. For a while she got nightly phone calls from her father, but gradually they diminished. A year later, Mr. Makharis married a widow near his own age, who shares his interest in bowling and clerks on occasion in the hardware store. Grace was proud to be maid of honor at the wedding.

MR. AND MISS RESPONSIBILITY

In Grace's situation her father had indeed fostered and encouraged the feeling that she was responsible for him.

More commonly in this country children contribute to (and perhaps create) a sense of being responsible for their parents. If you're living at home with parents it's very easy to become far over worried about their aging, and all of us have been too well taught how to go on a guilt trip; we easily fall into the trap of feeling we have to take care of them. Most parents, even if they have some significant physical problem, are much less aware of changes in their ability to function. They feel (and are) quite competent to care for themselves.

A young person's sense of having to take responsibility usually develops so gradually that he or she has little awareness of where it came from and never bothers to check it out. If you feel this kind of responsibility to the extent that it would deter you from accepting an otherwise attractive relocation, we advise you to check it out.

Sit your parents down and tell them what you feel. Try to pin down for yourself why you feel it. Ask them to respond. Ask directly if they feel a need to have you take care of them. Separate this from whether they feel they would like to have you continue living home or close by. That's totally different from a need to be taken care of.

ISSUES FOR OTHER SINGLES

Many singles, who have been living away from home and long established a working relationship with their parents, may still have difficulty putting down roots in a new community.

They must combine a full-time job with all the housekeeping chores and without the help or emotional support of a spouse. Married people tend to underestimate how much harder this is for the single person without the structure, chore cooperation and incentive that a husband or wife provides. It's sometimes very difficult to find the motivation to clean, cook tempting meals or food shop with enthusiasm if there is no one to share in the outcome. And the physical burden is just as rough as it is for the working spouse who comes home to begin another set of chores. Dual career families usually agree to some splitting of labors.

Singles should acknowledge all this and should level with the people around them. Far too often people diminish these concerns of singles.

Maggie Thomas is twenty-nine, never married and has hired someone to help with the chores. But she's a little defensive about it.

"Nellie comes in two days a week," she says. "She cleans,

shops and generally keeps my life in order. I get a lot of criticism from my married friends about having her. *They* don't have help and can't understand why a single woman, with only herself to look after, needs a maid.

"Well, I *do* need somebody. I work hard. I'm at the office at 9:00 and don't get home often till 6:30 or 7:00—exhausted. Nobody would criticize my having someone come in if I were a *man!*"

AND HOW ABOUT THE SOCIAL LIFE?

This is a sticky subject for singles of both sexes.

Some married men and women, along with TV, Hollywood and defensive singles, would have us all believe that the singles scene is really swinging, a wild and fun place to be. Getting dates and companionship is supposedly a cinch. Being able to go out any night, go anyplace you want, not be tied down to a wife or husband waiting for you at a certain time—that's real freedom.

Relocation is just a lot of fun for the single person, right? After all it's a new opportunity to try the field and social offerings of a new place.

That's not at all what the singles in our groups report. They talk about how hard it is to make new friends and how they have to search for places they feel safe going alone. They talk about how much easier it is for married people with children to find friends and activities. Married people can use the children as a matrix from which it's safe to extend themselves into exploring who to befriend. They're invited to PTA meetings. They're usually sought after to help with the scouts and Brownies, soccer, Little League and so on. Singles do not have that ready-made entrance to a community, and it can be rough to get established.

Andy Ames, twenty-eight, and recently transferred, describes himself as "the loneliest guy in town. Where can a single guy go to meet people, except bars? And that's just not my scene. And don't tell me about newcomers clubs. Newcomers clubs are all married people, and they're only interested in meeting other couples.

Audrey Miller, also twenty-eight and transferred, smiled ruefully when she heard Andy's story. "I can go him one better," she said. "I lucked out at newcomers club, too. Everybody just stared at me as if I'm some creature from outer space. Andy at least can ask women he meets through work for dates. I have to wait for the men to ask me. Believe me, I spend a lot of lonely evenings watching TV."

We believe her. The unfortunate fact is that most newcomers clubs and similar organizations established to make new arrivals in the community feel at home are overwhelmingly made up of couples, and couples do gravitate toward other couples.

Singles should still make the effort to join groups, but different kinds of groups. Joining a church or a synagogue is an excellent way to meet people, married and single. Religious organizations also usually sponsor activities groups, volunteer groups and committees that members are welcome to join. Working together with people on behalf of a good cause is a great way to make friends.

Special interest groups can work wonders for you. What's your hobby? What are you good at—or what would you like to learn to be good at? Whether it's backgammon or bowling, soccer or stamp collecting, in most good sized communities you'll find some like-minded enthusiasts. Join up! Why be shy about it? You're there not primarily to meet people, but because of your interest in the activity. Still, meeting people is an inevitable by-product.

Last but hardly least, how about taking some courses? This is an especially good idea for young, single transferees. Remember all the friends you made in high school and college? Well, you can do it all over again with people of your own age in night extension classes.

We feel that we all have a responsibility to acknowledge what it's like for singles to move into a community; married couples need to help out. Instead of feeling threatened and keeping singles that move into your neighborhood at arm's length, give them a chance, invite them as you might a new married couple who moved in and convey support for their adjustment period when they're new in town.

HOW ABOUT LEAVING FRIENDS?

Most people easily empathize when married couples mourn the disruption of friendships, but what about our "carefree" unattached singles? In fact, friendships for single people may be more critical to their sense of security, their sense of fulfillment and meaning in their lives. Don't forget, they do not have a spouse to talk to, fight with, or cry to when in pain and laugh with when joyful. The sense of camaraderie among singles is often intense; leaving these relationships can be a most difficult and frightening experience.

If you're single, you need to discuss the transfer offer openly with your friends. Acknowledge to yourself how you feel. Be sure to express to them what you feel and get their reactions. They probably love you and do not want you to leave because of normally selfish reasons, but you need to know how they feel.

The fear of not being able to make new friends is natural. However, the best indication that you can do so is that you presently have friends. You did it once, you can again.

DIVORCED WITH CHILDREN?

A divorced person's biggest barrier to accepting a transfer often involves children. "How can I leave my children?" or "What will it do to my children?" We hear these questions often from divorced people in our workshops. There is no way around the pain of moving 900 miles away from your children and facing the thought of probably seeing them only two or three times a year. It's a decision that only you can make and whether it's right or wrong for you is totally an individual matter. What we can do is help you understand the issues involved and offer some ways of handling the new situation if you accept the transfer.

What's at Stake?

Children through their teens need to have a relationship with both parents if at all possible. The relationships provide identifications (models) for the child, a sense of security and a reasonable measure of predictability. It is very important that a child feel that his or her own private world is not going to be disrupted by a parent's move.

Children want to know that someone is there for them if they need help. They thrive on any signals that convey: "I'm wanted, I'm loved, I'm needed." The worst thing would be somehow to make them feel guilty. Guilt cannot be constructive. It can only give the youngsters ammunition, so your move and their adjustment will become as difficult as possible.

What Can You Do?

Be sure you know why you're accepting the move and spell it out to them very clearly. Don't make up stories. Be honest. Children can usually accept rational explanations, and while they may feel bad they'll at least know you care enough about them to level with them. Do not approach the talk hoping for smiles or consoling words from them to make you feel better. Somebody (probably everybody) needs to feel bad about daddy moving away, but these are normal healthy responses; allow them to get expressed.

You should be very explicit about where you will be; how you will live; and how you will keep the relationship going. In as many ways as possible, you must convey that geographical distance will not become emotional distance.

Set up a schedule of phone calls so they know you will call on a certain night each week and at a certain time. Stick with that agreement no matter what.

Agree to exchange tape recordings on a regular basis. This can be a very effective and informed way of keeping up family jokes and interests. Children need to feel that the familiar continues to be a tie between them and the parent, so don't be afraid to bring up pleasant incidents from the past or nonsense things that went on between you. The key is to communicate that there will be stability in the relationship and your emotional ties to the children despite the distance.

You have to convince yourself that you will not permit geographical distance to dilute your involvement with them or the joint decision-making about their lives that goes on between you and their mother.

It's also critical to assure them of visits with you on whatever schedule is feasible. This is important enough to justify a significant financial sacrifice.

What About the Divorced Woman?

Now that more women are being transferred, the situation of the divorced mother (who most of the time has custody of the children) taking them many miles from daddy is becoming more common. The same guidelines as spelled out for the divorced male apply. The children's needs remain the same. The added complication is that they are being relocated themselves, and that has plus and minus aspects. Some children go through geographical separations from the father easier because they do not feel that he is rejecting them. They're the ones who are moving, and mother made the choice. In other cases they feel some of the same guilt that the father might feel in accepting a transfer.

In either situation it's important to provide ways for the children to keep in contact with the distant parent and to help them do it. It is critical that the divorced couple bury the hatchet so that they can cooperate in making a plan for the children.

The decision to transfer if you're divorced and have children is not easy; you might do well to seek a professional briefing about it once or twice. If you must leave children, we can't overemphasize that you must make them aware of how you feel about them and leaving them.

TO GET RELIABLE CHILD CARE

When a single parent moves and has children with him, care for those children becomes the primary concern.

The Proxy Grandmother

Many a lonely widow who lives on social security or a tiny pension and would never dream of being somebody's maid is most amenable to the role of proxy grandmother. It is a way of using the only skills she knows—homemaking and mothering—to earn money and reap the emotional bonus of a new, substitute family.

Proxy grandmothers do light housework, care for children during the day, take meals with the employer, share in the cooking and in the evening baby-sitting. In short, they fill exactly the role that many real grandmothers do—except that they don't live with the employer and have Saturdays and Sundays off. The best way to find a proxy grandmother is through an ad posted on a church or retirement home bulletin board or placed in a local paper.

The Mother's Pool

This takes a bit of arranging, but it has been worked out successfully by many groups of women. Typically, five or six women with children, some with jobs and some without, set up a mutual baby-sitting arrangement. These can vary according to the ages and number of children involved as well as the schedules of the mothers, but generally it works like this.

The stay-at-home mothers take over the after school detail. For example, the children go after school to the homes of one or another of the non-working mothers and stay there until their own mothers come to pick them up. The working mothers bear the major responsibility for evening hour child care.

The system has many advantages. No money changes hands; it's a good example of the bartering of services. The parents are sure that their children are being left in good hands. Not the least, this is a way for the transferred divorced mother—and her children—to make new friends.

Of course there's no rule that says that a divorced father caring for children can't participate in such an arrangement, too.

WHERE TO LIVE

This can be a significant problem for the single person. Many (if not most) single working people can't take on the care of a house, with its yardwork, maintenance and repairs. So many singles choose to live in a condominium complex, where they pay monthly maintenance fees for services that do-it-yourself homeowners do themselves (lawn mowing, garden tending, painting and repairs to the outside of the building, and the like).

A good sized condominium complex usually has workers who, for a small fee, do indoor repairs for owners. At the least, the condominium manager can tell a newly transferred owner how and where to find a reliable plumber or electrician quickly. Which is no small service. It's a way of plugging into a community within a community.

Remember: there are different kinds of condominium arrangements, and this is something to discuss with your relocation director or company designated realtor if you're thinking of buying a condominium apartment.

Some are segregated by age and marital status. There are condominiums for young singles; condominiums for retired people; condominiums for families. This is usually not a matter of house rules; it's just that like tends to congregate with like, and as newcomers buy into the complex, it takes on a definite character.

Many condominiums and apartments are mixed: older people, young people, single people, married people and people with children of all ages. These are a particularly good choice for the young adult with a child or children. There are, right on the premises, potential proxy grandmas (or grandpas), teen-age or college age helpers, and other mothers to form mothers' pools with. In addition, it enables the single parent and child to live in an environment with a cross section of neighbors of all ages. Healthy for the child, certainly— and for the parent as well.

WHEN YOU'RE LIVING TOGETHER

Twenty years ago this wasn't usually a discussable solution. Transferees were either married or single. Now, when half of an unmarried couple is transferred it can create a problem. It can also help to solve a deeper one.

It's hardly necessary to point out that companies *do not* regard live in women or men companions as spouses. If Mary wishes to follow John to his new location, that's her project; John's company is not going to pay her expenses. The need to make such a decision can, however, help such a couple to clarify their relationship.

Carrie Marcus and Dan Timm, twenty-six and thirty, had been sharing an apartment for four years when Dan was transferred to another city. There was no question of Dan's turning down a transfer; the move was too important to his career.

"What about me?" Carrie asked.

"Well," said Dan. "Do you want to come along? You'd have to get another job out there, of course, but we could still go along just the way we're going."

"I don't know" said Carrie.

Carrie and Dan sat down and asked themselves some hard questions.

Do we want to stay together permanently? Or do we want to reserve the option of seeing other people?

How important is the untransferred partner's (Carrie's) job?

Do we want, eventually, to marry?

Do we want children?

Where is this relationship going?

In the case of Carrie and Dan, it wasn't going anywhere.

"It was just a holding operation, I guess," Carrie admitted. "Yes, my job is important to me. I don't want to go chasing Dan all over the country. I do want to marry some day but not Dan. He's a lot of fun, but I'd like to get to know more men first."

And from Dan: "Carrie's right. It was a holding operation, we had a lot of fun and I'll sure miss her but I'm ready now to settle down, marry and have children. She's not.

"The relationship was falling apart anyway, for all these reasons. For better or worse, my transfer brought things to a point, and we were forced to settle it. And a good thing! We could have gone on and on being roommates until we were both too old to establish other lives for ourselves."

Mildred Macy and Ed Grant, aged twenty-nine and thirty-four, had lived together for six years when Ed was transferred. They were confronted by the same problem. They asked themselves the same questions, but came up with quite different answers. They did want to stay together permanently. They could not, in fact, imagine life without each other. Mildred, a secretary, saw no problem in finding work in Ed's new area. And both wanted very much to start a family.

"And so we did the obvious thing," said Ed. "We got married. Why didn't we think of it before? Well, we weren't that sure six years ago.

"But even though it's still not socially acceptable in some circles, I'll say one thing for living together. We know each other really well. We've long since adjusted to each other's little idiosyncracies. We're a good working team and best friends as well as lovers.

"Maybe we waited a long time to make it legal, but we both know exactly what we're getting into. There's a pretty slim chance of *our* ever ending up in the divorce court."

IT'S IN YOUR HEAD

Bob Sarron was being transferred. He had sailed smoothly through the phases of being told about the transfer, the policy presentation (his company did not offer financial counseling and he did nothing to seek it), and the initial stage of home selling. No negative feelings.

The day before he was to have his area counseling meeting (see following chart) the first real estate appraiser, whom he and the relocation management company had agreed on came to his home. Diane, his wife, was home alone. Through some mix-up of signals she was not expecting the appraiser. The house was not picked up. She really resented his looking into her closets and hit the ceiling when he began to ask who built the cabinets in the family room.

For whatever reason, the appraiser commented about the amateurish workmanship of the job in a relatively hostile way and suggested that the level of the carpentry would make the house a little more difficult to market. As you can guess, Bob and Diane had worked together many evenings creating these bookshelves and cabinets.

The next day, in the area consultant's office, Diane had very little to say. The consultant was unable to get Diane to describe what kind of house—or even what kind of community—she was looking for. Diane had been very hurt by

Relocation Process

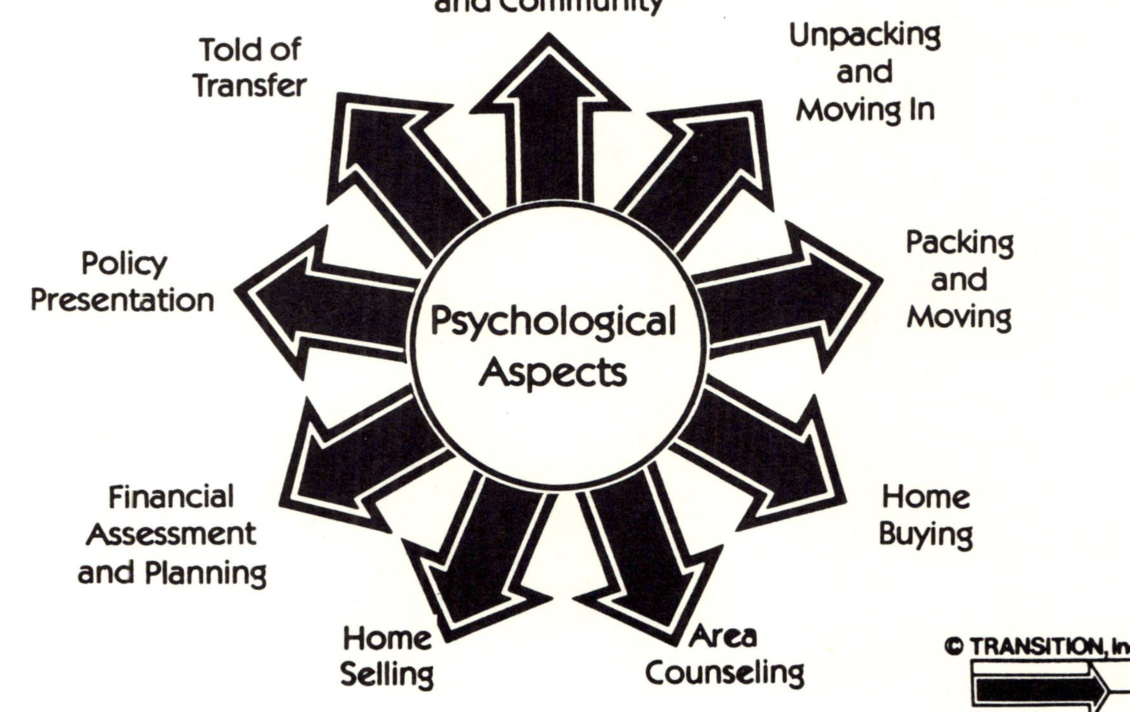

the appraiser's comments. Her psychological makeup had caused her to equate the appraiser with outsiders having control of moving, home selling and buying.

The area consultant was bewildered. In a training seminar we ran for her company she told the Sarrons' story and added, "I spent over one hour trying to pull from this lady something about her that would help me counsel them. After I threw up my hands, Mr. Sarron finally told me about the appraiser. I felt like I was hit with a hammer. It was pure chance that he told me. From that point on I was able to work with the couple."

No one working with a transferee and his or her family can afford to ignore any phase of a move. Everyone must develop ways to learn diplomatically what a transferee and/or his family has experienced during a relocation.

Psychological is a big word, but it has a lot to do with tactless appraisers. Also with other emotions, thoughts, attitudes, wishes, values, motivations, interpersonal and inter-family relationships, and feelings one has about oneself. Psychology governs us, makes up our decisions and is responsible for everything we do. It comes into play in every significant event, and who can doubt that relocation is a significant event?

Relocation is not one act, obviously. It's a sequence and is relatively predictable. To cope with one stage of the sequence if you've not successfully completed previous stages (or if you're still sulking about a nasty appraiser) is futile.

Dr. Edgar Mitchell, one of the astronaut pioneers who traveled to the moon, addressing the 1980 Employee Relocation Council meeting, cautioned everyone to remember that relocation is not different from anything else. We create our own reality. If you come to a new community, he said, you bring along your expectations and often create the scene you wind up in.

We agree. Yet people under stress frequently have difficulty creating their reality and are prone to misinterpret. Bob Sarron's rude appraiser did not reflect how Bob's company felt. So you may need some help to create the best possible new situation for yourself. We hope you find it in this book. And don't be embarrassed or bashful about asking for more help and accepting it.

Relocation can be a positive life experience. Corporations, the relocation industry, communities, and you, the transferee, can make it that way. It won't happen by magic—or by sulking and clamming up. But the resources exist to make moving exciting: resources of the corporations, relocation firms, your family, your friends, churches and synagogues, professionals and yourselves. Use them and good luck!

APPENDICES

RELOCATION MANAGEMENT COMPANIES

Bank of Oklahoma, N.A.
P. O. Box 2300
Tulsa, Oklahoma 74192
(918) 588–6435
Ms. Sue White, Trust Officer

Bank of St. Louis
901 Washington Avenue
St. Louis, Missouri 63101
(314) 241–3600
John R. Kovach, Vice-President, Home Management Department

Charter Equities, Inc.
1819 Lee Avenue
Sanford, North Carolina 27330
(919) 776–6841
Dempsey M. Jones

Employee Transfer Corporation
20 North Wacker Drive
Chicago, Illinois 60606
(312) 630–2980
E. William McCarty, Manager of Home Purchase Operations

Equitable Relocation Service
1221 Avenue of the Americas
New York, New York 10020
(212) 354–4500
James P. Walsh, Jr., Director, Relocation Operations

Executive Relocation Corp.
26111 Woodward Ave.
Chamberlain Bldg.
Huntington Woods, Missouri 48070
(313) 541–1600
Del Warner, Vice-President

Executrans, Inc.
102 Wilmot Road
Deerfield, Illinois 60015
(312) 948–7000
Al DeCesare, Assistant Vice-President/Operations

First National Bank in Bartlesville
121 West 4th Street,
P. O. Box 999
Bartlesville, Oklahoma 74003
(918) 336–6121
Felix Roquemore, Real Property Manager

First Tennessee Bank N.A., Memphis
P. O. Box 84
Memphis, Tennessee 38101
(901) 523–4512
B. Mott Jones, Manager/Employee Relocation Service

Homequity, Inc.
249 Danbury Road
Wilton, Connecticut 06897
(203) 762–2281
James M. Keane, Vice-President

Merrill Lynch Relocation Management, Inc.
4 Corporate Park Drive
White Plains, New York 10604
(914) 694–8484
John M. Moore, Vice-President

Midlantic Mortgage Corp.
60 Park Place
Newark, New Jersey 07102
(201) 624-8700
Richard L. Bartsch
Vice-President/Home Sales Division

Potere, Inc.
470 Elmore Avenue
Elizabeth, New Jersey 07208
(201) 354-4481
E. M. Mansfield, Vice-President

RELCO, Inc.
1401 Walnut Street
Philadelphia, Pennsylvania 19102
(215) 563-9482
William A. Cordivari

Relocation Realty Service Corporation
733 Third Avenue
New York, New York 10017
(212) 661-7337
Arnold Wells, Vice-President

Republic National Bank of Dallas
P. O. Box 241
Dallas, Texas 75221
(214) 653-6535
J. Michael Chastain, Vice-President

Texas Commerce Bank N.A.
712 Main Street
Houston, Texas 77002
(713) 236-4550
Ms. Barbara A. Garren

Transamerica Relocation Service, Inc.
1900 North California Blvd.
Walnut Creek, California 94596
(415) 943-5200
C. Douglas Shepard, Vice-President/Operations

VanRelco, Inc.
1515 Arapahoe
Denver, Colorado 80202
(303) 573–6563
Ms. Jean Jones, Vice-President/Operations

Wachovia Bank & Trust Co., N.A.
400 South Tryon Street
Charlotte, North Carolina 28231
(704) 378–5495
Ms. Lyn B. Hudson

The following relocation (home purchase) companies are located in Canada:

A. E. LePage, Ltd.
50 Holly Street
Toronto, Ontario M4S 2G1
Canada
(416) 484–6141
Mr. Julian Merry, Vice-President

Relocan, Ltd.
43 Eglinton Avenue East, Suite 700
Toronto, Ontario M4P 1A2
Canada
(416) 485–6591
Ms. Susan M. O'Dell, Director of Relocation Services

National Trust
101 Queensway West, 5th Floor
Mississauga, Ontario L5B 1P7
Canada
(416) 276–4150
Mr. A. J. McArthur, Manager, Relocation Department

THE ABC'S OF HOUSE HUNTING

Once you have a feel for the community, you'll need to focus in on the house. Use a realtor. Since the seller pays the commission, you get the advantage of a professional who can provide you with a great deal of information at no charge to you, the buyer.

Setting

The home you buy should fit naturally into the neighborhood and blend in price and style with the surrounding homes. It should look as though it belongs on the lot and in the neighborhood. It's wise to choose the lowest-priced, smallest home in the area. Then the other homes will pull up your home's value as they appreciate.

Your Requirements

Decide beforehand what you absolutely require and what is flexible. Don't be swayed by a charming, three bedroom home when you require four bedrooms. If a family room is important to you, look until you find one. If you let your emotions buy the house, you may be sorry six months later.

Ask Questions

Above all, ask questions. Ask your realtor, the owner, and the listing agent about the home. Ask about the tax bill, utility costs, the reasons for selling, the condition of all major systems and appliances. Then test the answers. Look for signs of leaks and dampness. Check the water pressure. There's a difference between being inquisitive and being a cautious potential buyer. It's your money, so don't be embarrassed.

Be Honest

Be honest to yourself and your realtor. The only way your realtor can help is if you react naturally to the homes shown. What you don't like is almost as important as what you liked about a home. This helps eliminate homes with similar shortcomings. Be honest about your price range. Don't overextend or settle for less than you require.

Keeping Track of the Houses

Don't try to remember more than four homes. Measure each home against the best four. Eliminate as you go. Get a copy of the listing. Use a checklist to keep notes on the homes you've seen.

HOME CHECKLIST

Consider:

Setting

Age of home

Property taxes

Number of bedrooms

Size of bedrooms

Number of baths and location

Dining area or separate room

Separate entrance hall

Functional kitchen

Adequate cabinet space

Condition of appliances included in sale

Adequate counter space

Condition of kitchen floor

Is there enough wall space for furniture & wall hangings?

Amount and quality of carpeting

Type of floors

Adequate closets and storage

Basement, crawl space, attic storage

Size of garage

Laundry facilities

Type of heat and yearly cost

Adequate insulation

Does home have 220 volts?

Are there enough electrical outlets?

Are there city sewers or septic?

Is water supply city or well?

Is the pressure adequate?

Is there enough hot water?

Do you need a water softener?

Are there enough windows?

Are windows and doors weatherstripped?

Are there storms and screens?

Is the roof in good shape?

Are there gutters?

Is siding of good quality?

Does the home need painting?

HOW TO SELECT A COMMUNITY

Location, Location, Location

You are buying a community, not just a home. Your choice is critical to both the home's future investment potential and to its livability. A listing of some of the things that will help you select a community.

Character

The total visual impression of an area is a true indication of the community's personality. Look for a neighborhood that is stabilized or, even better, improving. Make sure it is not deteriorating.

Look for care and pride of ownership. Beware of too many "for sale" signs or a neighborhood with many homes for rent.

During your tour of the area, take a deep breath. Is the air clean? Smog problems are worse in some areas than others. Listen too. How noisy is it? Is there a factory, airport, or major freeway intersection nearby? Look for cul-de-sacs and dead ends for safety and quieter living.

Zoning

Ordinances are legislated by local governments and are intended to promote uniformity among general building characteristics within an area. By regulating what can and cannot be built, residential neighborhoods are protected against unwanted or poorly located commercial development. The zoning classification of nearby undeveloped land is important, too. Today's empty fields could be tomorrow's schools, shopping centers, or parking lots. Carefully zoned areas tend to hold their property values. This can be important when it comes time to sell.

Convenience

Consider the distance and time to work. Make a trial run over the commuter's route during rush hour before you decide on a location. A quick drive around the area will give you a fair picture of what is and is not within reasonable distance. Make sure you and your family will be comfortable with the areas conveniences or isolation.

Services

Don't underestimate the importance of essential services. Water, natural gas, police and fire protection, sewer systems, garbage collection, and snow removal can certainly affect the livability of an area. Check into the recreational and cultural facilities available in the area. Are there enough tennis courts, public swimming facilities, adult education courses and colleges nearby? How about a newcomer's club to help you get established?

The quality of schools can vary tremendously from one district to another. Visit the school, talk to the principal. What is the average class size? Are there split sessions? Ask how much is spent on education per student and how the taxpayers have voted on school budgets. Find out how active the school's extracurricular program is. A few visits and phone calls can help you separate rumors and opinions from fact. Remember that if schools are unimportant to you they may not be to the future buyer of your home.

Property Taxes

All these facilities and services cost money. Find out what you will be paying for them and whether you will get your money's worth. After your mortgage bill, your tax bill is likely to be your second biggest home ownership cost. Are the real estate assessments and taxes recalculated at the time of sale? If so, taxes may be much higher than the previous owner paid. Check for special assessments too. If the town is growing quickly, so may your taxes.

After considering all these points carefully, you will be ready to start searching for a specific home. Use the following checklist and remember "location, location, location." Those are the three most important factors in selecting an area and home to live in.

COMMUNITY CHECKLIST

Is the community attractive?

Are the homes well maintained?

How is the area zoned?

Is land and home value increasing?

Are good public schools available?

COMMUNITY CHECKLIST (continued)

How much will the yearly property, sales, and income taxes be?

How many miles to work?

What will monthly commutation costs be?

Are there cultural, educational & medical facilities?

Is there adequate water supply?

What type of fire protection?

Is there adequate police protection?

Does the community provide garbage removal, snow removal, sewers, drains?

Are there recreational and play areas nearby?

What are traffic conditions?

Are there any objectionable noises or smells?

How far are shopping, theaters, libraries?

YOUR HOUSEHOLD INVENTORY

The following is an inventory for recording your household furnishings and personal inventory. It is important that you have a record of your possessions and their value. We hope this form will be helpful in compiling this record.

Article	How Many	Year Bought	Cost	Present Value
Living room				
Chairs				
Tables				
Davenport				
Rugs				
Carpet				

YOUR HOUSEHOLD INVENTORY (continued)

Article	How Many	Year Bought	Cost	Present Value
Lamps				
Pictures				
Mirrors				
Piano				
Organ				
Radio				
Clock				
Curtains				
Draperies				
Fireplace Fittings				
Vases				
TV Set				
Record Player				
Records				
Hi-Fi				
Stereo				

YOUR HOUSEHOLD INVENTORY (continued)

Article	How Many	Year Bought	Cost	Present Value
TOTAL LIVING ROOM				

Family room

Article	How Many	Year Bought	Cost	Present Value
Chairs				
Tables				
Desks				
Sofa				
Rugs				
Carpet				
Lamps				
Pictures				

YOUR HOUSEHOLD INVENTORY *(continued)*

Article	How Many	Year Bought	Cost	Present Value
Radio				
Record Player				
Mirrors				
Clock				
Bookcases				
Curtains				
Draperies				
TV Set				
Stereo				
Bar				
Ping Pong Table				
Pool Table				
Games				
TOTAL FAMILY ROOM				

Dining room

Table				
Chairs				

YOUR HOUSEHOLD INVENTORY *(continued)*

Article	How Many	Year Bought	Cost	Present Value
China Cabinet				
Buffet				
Server				
Tea Cart				
Rugs				
Carpet and Pad				
Curtains				
Draperies				
Pictures				
Mirrors				
Dinner Sets				
China				
Glassware				
		TOTAL DINING ROOM		

Bathrooms

YOUR HOUSEHOLD INVENTORY *(continued)*

Article	How Many	Year Bought	Cost	Present Value
	TOTAL BATHROOMS			

Bedroom 1

Article	How Many	Year Bought	Cost	Present Value
Beds				
Springs				
Mattresses				
Chests				
Chairs				
Vanities				
Dressing Tables				
Clocks				
Rugs				
Carpets				
Lamps				
Pictures				
Bedside Tables				
Curtains				
Draperies				
Radios				
	TOTAL BEDROOM 1			

YOUR HOUSEHOLD INVENTORY (continued)

Article	How Many	Year Bought	Cost	Present Value
Bedroom 2				
Beds				
Springs				
Mattresses				
Chests				
Chairs				
Vanities				
Dressing Tables				
Clocks				
Rugs				
Carpets				
Lamps				
Pictures				
Bedside Tables				
Curtains				
Draperies				
Radios				
		TOTAL BEDROOM 2		

Article	How Many	Year Bought	Cost	Present Value
Bedrooms 3, 4, 5				
Beds				

YOUR HOUSEHOLD INVENTORY *(continued)*

Article	How Many	Year Bought	Cost	Present Value
Springs				
Mattresses				
Chests				
Chairs				
Vanities				
Dressing Tables				
Clocks				
Rugs				
Carpets				
Lamps				
Pictures				
Bedside Tables				
Curtains				
Draperies				
Radios				

YOUR HOUSEHOLD INVENTORY *(continued)*

Article	How Many	Year Bought	Cost	Present Value
TOTAL BEDROOMS 3, 4, 5				

Kitchen

Article	How Many	Year Bought	Cost	Present Value
Refrigerator				
Range				
Deep Freeze				
Floor Covering				
Curtains				
Chairs				
Tables				
Utensils				
Dishes				
Supplies				
Radios				
Dishwasher				
TOTAL KITCHEN				

YOUR HOUSEHOLD INVENTORY (continued)

Article	How Many	Year Bought	Cost	Present Value
Laundry				
Washer				
Dryer				
Ironer				
Tables				
Electric Irons				
Dehumidifier				
	TOTAL LAUNDRY			
Lawn Furniture				
Chairs				
Tables				
Couch				
Glider				
Swing				
Gym Set				
Barbecue				
	TOTAL LAWN FURNITURE			

YOUR HOUSEHOLD INVENTORY (continued)

Article	How Many	Year Bought	Cost	Present Value
Machinery				
Sewing Machine				
Vacuum Cleaners				
Woodworking Equip.				
Power Tools				
		TOTAL MACHINERY		
Hand Tools				
Saws				
Drills				
		TOTAL HAND TOOLS		
Garden Tools				
Lawn Mowers				

YOUR HOUSEHOLD INVENTORY *(continued)*

Article	How Many	Year Bought	Cost	Present Value
Wheelbarrow				
Hand Tools				
Garden Hose				
	TOTAL GARDEN TOOLS			
Musical Instruments				
	TOTAL MUSICAL INSTRUMENTS			
Furs				
Coats				
Cape				
Stole				
	TOTAL FURS			

YOUR HOUSEHOLD INVENTORY *(continued)*

Article	How Many	Year Bought	Cost	Present Value

Clothing

Men's

Women's

YOUR HOUSEHOLD INVENTORY *(continued)*

Article	How Many	Year Bought	Cost	Present Value
Children's				
		TOTAL CLOTHING		

Article	How Many	Year Bought	Cost	Present Value
Linens				
Sheets				
Pillow Cases				
Blankets				
Spreads				
Table Cloths				
Napkins				
Luncheon Sets				
Towels				
Wash Cloths				

YOUR HOUSEHOLD INVENTORY (continued)

Article	How Many	Year Bought	Cost	Present Value
Bath Mats				
		TOTAL LINENS		
Jewelry				
Watches				
Rings				
Necklaces				
Bracelets				
Brooches				
		TOTAL JEWELRY		
Silver				
Holloware				
Silverware				
Tea Set				
Trays				

YOUR HOUSEHOLD INVENTORY (continued)

Article	How Many	Year Bought	Cost	Present Value
		TOTAL SILVER		

Personal Belongings

Sports Equipment

Guns

Luggage

Stamp, Coin Collection

Bicycles

Toys

	TOTAL PERSONAL BELONGINGS			

YOUR HOUSEHOLD INVENTORY *(continued)*

Article	How Many	Year Bought	Cost	Present Value
Miscellaneous				
	TOTAL MISCELLANEOUS			

SUMMARY OF VALUATION

	Present Value
Living room	
Family room	
Dining room	
Bathrooms	
Bedroom 1	
Bedroom 2	
Bedrooms 3, 4, 5	
Kitchen	
Laundry	
Lawn Furniture	
Machinery	
Hand Tools	
Garden Tools	
Musical Instruments	
Furs	
Clothing	
Linens	
Jewelry	
Silver	
Personal Belongings	
Miscellaneous	
VALUE TOTAL	

Travel expenses

Travel expenses

TOTAL TRAVEL EXPENSES

Moving expenses

TOTAL MOVING EXPENSE

Miles moved

Weight of move

Packing charges

Notes for next time you move:

Picture of old home

Picture of new home

BIBLIOGRAPHY

Selected Supplementary Reading
(General)

BOOKS

Bird, Caroline. *The Two Paycheck Marriage.* New York: Rawson, Wade Publishers, Inc., 1979

> Insightful observations on dual-career couples and how they work out their problems.

Bird, Caroline. *Everything a Woman Needs to Know to Get Paid What She's Worth.* New York: Bantam Books, 1974.

> Just what the title says it is. Thought provoking for the woman on her way up in business.

Bolles, Richard Nelson. *What Color Is Your Parachute?* Berkeley, California: Ten Speed Press, 1972.

> Helpful and inspirational best-seller. For men and women seeking to find (or change) jobs.

Feinberg, Morton, Ph.D. *Corporate Bigamy—How To Resolve the Conflict between Career and Family.* New York: William Morrow and Co., 1980.

Forbes, Rosalind, Ed. D. *Corporate Stress.* Garden City, New York: Doubleday & Company, Inc., 1979.

Friedan, Betty. *The Feminine Mystique.* New York: W. W. Norton & Company, 1963.

 Landmark study of the dissatisfied housewife that launched the women's movement.

Glazer, Nathan, and Moynihan, Daniel P. *Beyond the Melting Pot.* Massachusetts Institute of Technology Press, 1963.

 Scholarly (and controversial) study of America's ethnic minorities.

Hall, Francine S., and Hall, Douglas T. *The Two-Career Couple.* Reading, Massachusetts: Addison-Wesley Publishing Company, 1979.

Harrigan, Betty Lehan. *Games Mother Never Taught You.* New York: Rawson Associates, 1977.

 Hardheaded, tough talking advice to women on how to make it up the corporate ladder.

Janeway, Elizabeth. *Man's World, Woman's Place.* New York: William Morrow, Inc., 1973.

 Thoughtful, beautifully written book on the changing roles of the sexes.

Kanter, Rosabeth Moss. *Men and Women of the Corporation.* New York: Basic Books, Inc. 1977.

 Scholarly but highly readable study of life within the corporation today.

Korda, Michael. *Male Chauvinism! How It Works.* New York: Random House, 1973.

 Witty inside information for women (and men) who want to know.

Margolis, Diane Rothbard. *The Managers Corporate Life in America.* New York: William Morrow & Company, 1979.

Parkard, Vance. *A Nation of Strangers.* New York: Pocket Books, 1974.

 A report on the new mobile society by the well-known social historian.

Seidenberg, Robert, *Corporate Wives, Corporate Casualties*. New York: American Management Association, Inc., 1973.

Some enlightened case studies by a psychoanalyst.

Shaevitz, Marjorie and Shaevitz, Morton. *Making It Together As a Two Career Couple*. Boston, Massachusetts: Houghton Miflin Company, 1980.

Tiger, Lionel. *Men in Groups*. New York: Random House, 1969.

How (and why) men stick together.

Toffler, Alvin. *Future Shock*. New York: Random House, 1970, Bantam, 1971.

Provocative predictions on our rapidly changing society.

Walters, Barbara. *How to Talk with Practically Anybody About Practically Anything*. New York: Dell, 1970.

Chatty, entertaining tips on making friends by the well known TV newswoman.

Welch, Mary Scott. *Networking*. New York: Harcourt Brace Jovanovich, 1980.

How women are finding (and forming) groups to make business contacts and pool job finding information, with seven page nationwide directory of such groups.

Whyte, William H. *The Organization Man*. New York: Simon and Schuster, 1956. Touchstone Books, Simon and Schuster, 1972.

Landmark study of the male executive.

FREE BOOKLETS AND PAMPHLETS

Internal Revenue Service Publication 521 (10–72)
"Tax Information on Moving Expenses." May be obtained from your nearest I.R.S. office

Interstate Commerce Commission free publications:
"Loss and Damage Claims . . . Can You Collect?"

"Lost or Damaged Household Goods"
"Small Shipments"
"Top Twenty Carriers and Their Performance Ratings for the Past Year"
"Summary of Information for Shippers of Household Goods"

To obtain: call the ICC toll-free number: 800-424-9312 or write,

> Interstate Commerce Commission
> Consumer Assistance Branch
> Room 7309
> Washington, D.C. 20423

Many moving companies provide practical consumer information booklets. United Van Lines has an especially complete list. Titles include:

"Pre-Planned Moving Guide"
"Answers to Questions about Money"
"Tax Deductible Moving Expenses"
"Moving with Children"
"Moving with Pets"
"Moving with Houseplants"
"Preparing Appliances for Moving"
"Selling Your House"
"Buying a House"
"Pre-Planning a Garage Sale"
"Doing Your Own Packing"

These can be obtained without charge from local United Van Lines agents.

From local Allied Van Lines agents you can obtain without charge three basic guides:

"A Moving Story"
"The Helping Handbook"
"The Mover's Guide to Self-Packing"

SELECTED SUPPLEMENTARY READING
BY SUBJECT

(Courtesy: The Relocation Bibliography compiled by the Reference Committee, Reference and Adult Services Section, New York Public Library Association.)

Climate

Climates of the States. James Ruffner and Frank Blair, eds. Detroit, Mi., Gale Research, 1977. 2v.

Traveling Weatherwise in the U.S.A. Edward Powers and James Witt. New York. Dodd, Mead, 1972.
> Over 150 charts, giving the weather characteristics of cities all over the U.S., as well as 50 pages of maps discussing weather patterns and local conditions in each weather area.

Weather Almanac. Ruffner and Bair. 2nd ed. Detroit, Mi., Gale Research, 1977.
> A reference guide to weather and climate of the U.S. and its key cities. Includes reference data on storms and weather extremes. Also includes world climatological highlights.

Weather Atlas of the United States. U.S. Environmental Data Service. Detroit, Mi., Gale Research 1968 reprint 1975. Original title **Climate Atlas of the United States.**
> Depicts climate of U.S. in terms of distribution and variation of such climate measures as temperature precipitation, wind, barometric pressures, relative humidity, etc.

Weather Handbook. Conway and Liston. Rev. ed. Atlanta, Ga., Conway Research, 1977.
> A summary of weather statistics for principal cities throughout the U.S. and around the world. Charts & maps.

Crime

Almanacs
>**CBS News Almanac**
>**Information Please Almanac**
>**World Almanac and Book of Facts**
>These give crime rates by state: totals.

America's 50 Safest Cities. David Franke. New Rochelle, N.Y., Arlington House, 1974.
>Gives crime rates for all communities with a population of 50,000 or more; number of offenses in each crime category for 1970–71. Read introduction for best use of materials.

Crime in the United States. Washington, D.C., U.S. Department of Justice, Federal Bureau of Investigation, G.P.O.
>Annual. Includes all communities of 25,000 or more in population. This is the root source of all information on the subject.

Statistical Abstract of the United States. Washington, D.C., U.S. Census Bureau, Department of Commerce, G.P.O.
>Annual. Crime for 48 cities: police protection and fire protection.

Sourcebook of Criminal Justice Statistics. Michael J. Hindelang et al., Criminal Justice Research Center. Albany, N.Y. Washington, D.C., U.S. Department of Justice, G.P.O.
>Annual. Statistical coverage of criminal justice system, public attitudes, crime in selected cities.

Safe Places: East of the Mississippi. David Franke and Holly Franke. N.Y., Warner Books, 1973.

Cultural/Recreational

American Art Directory. 47th. ed. New York, Bowker, 1978.
>Title and frequency vary. Covers museums, art organizations, universities and colleges having art departments and museums of their own, art schools and classes in the

United States, Canada and abroad. In addition there are sections listing state art councils; art magazines; newspapers carrying art and their critics; traveling exhibitions with booking agencies and type of material and their sources and children's and junior museums.

The American Music Handbook. Christopher Pavlakis. New York, Free Press, 1974.

Intends to bring together information on all areas of organized musical activity in the United States. About 5,000 entries for service organizations and institutions, performing groups and ensembles, music societies, schools of music, music libraries and archives.

Campground and Trailer Park Guide. New York, Rand McNally & Co.

Annual. Covers the United States and Canada. Maps are accompanied by tables giving information on size, elevation, facilities, activities, etc.

Dance Magazine. New York, Danad Publishing Co.

Regular feature, Domestic Reports, provides information on a wide variety of dance activities in communities across the country.

Folk Dance Directory. Raymond La Barbara, ed. Brooklyn, N.Y., New York Folk Dance Association.

Annual. National listing of folk, square and round dancing with a classified directory.

Festivals U.S.A. and Canada. New York, Washburn.

Festivals are described under such groupings: agricultural festivals, beauty pageants, drama festivals, music festivals, sports festivals.

High Fidelity (magazine)—"Musical America" edition. New York, A.B.C. Leisure Magazines Inc.

The "Musical America" edition carries 32 extra pages which cover current music performances, music centers, and performing artists for those with a special interest in "live" music.

The Musician's Guide. Gladys S. Field. New York, Music Information Service, 1972.

Irregular. Offers directory information on music associations, competitions, awards, etc., education; libraries and publications; festivals; unions; and the music industry and trade.

National Directory for the Performing Arts and Civic Centers. Dallas, Tx., Handel & Co.

Annual. A listing by state, then by city, of performing arts organizations, with information on management, purpose, income sources, etc. College and university facilities are listed only when such institution has the major performance house for a surrounding area.

National Register of Historic Places. Washington, D.C., National Park Service.

Biennial. Describes places designated as national historic landmarks or preserved by the National Park Service with name, location, historical connection, etc. Geographical arrangement by state, then county.

New Woman's Survial Sourcebook. Susan Rennie and Kirsten Grimstad, eds., New York, Alfred A. Knopf. 1975.

A catalog of information on feminist communications, art, self-health, children, learning, self-defense, work, justice, and organizations and women's centers.

The Official Museum Directory: United States, Canada, Washington, D.C., Skokie, Il., American Association of Museums and National Register Publishing Co.

Povides information on 6,657 museums of art, history and science in four main sections: 1) institutions by state and province, 2) by name alphabetically, 3) by director and department heads alphabetically and 4) by category.

Opera News (magazine) New York, Metropolitan Opera Guild.

Two regular features provide information on the quantity and quality of operatic activity around the country. The U.S. Calendar lists operas (with casts) currently being performed by local opera companies nationwide.

Woodall's Trailering Parks and Campgrounds Directory. Highland Park, Il.

Annual. Covers United States, Canada and Mexico. Includes suggestions on planning trips.

Education

American Trade Schools Directory. Queens Village, N.Y., Croner, 1974.
> Subject & geographical listings.

American Art Directory. See: Cultural/Recreational.

College Guide for Students with Handicaps. See: Handicapped.

Directory of Educational Programs for the Gifted. Lavonne B. Axford. N.J., Scarecrow, 1971.
> Listing is by state. Includes both public and private institutions and summer programs.

The Directory for Exceptional Children. See: Handicapped.

The Directory of Facilities for the Learning-Disabled and Handicapped. See: Handicapped.

Directory of Public Elementary & Secondary Schools in Selected Districts. Enrollment and Staff by Racial/Ethnic Groups. Washington, D.C., U.S. Dept. of Health, Education and Welfare. Office of Civil Rights, 1972.

Directory of Schools and School Systems. Syracuse, N.Y. Gaylord Bros. 7 vols.
> Annual. All states and the District of Columbia are covered and are arranged alphabetically. Each state is sub-arranged by county. Within the county the list is by school district giving all public and parochial elementary and secondary schools. Information included is name and function of all chief officers and address, telephone, grades covered and enrollment of all schools.

Ed Fac Career School Directory: Business, Paraprofessional, Correspondence, Technical & Trade. Pekin, Il., Ed. Fac Publishing Co.
> Arranged by state with subject headings such as hairdressing, real estate and floral designs.

Educational Directory. Washington D.C., U.S. Office of Education. G.P.O.
> Annual. A useful annual varying in format and contents.

In four parts: State government, public school systems, higher education, and education associations.

A Handbook of Private Schools. Boston, Ma., Porter Sargent Publications Inc.
Annual.

Jewish Education Register and Directory. New York, American Association for Jewish Education.
A general section on various phases of Jewish education is followed by the directory, which includes educational agencies, schools, libraries, museums, summer camps, etc. Covers the United States and Canada.

Guide to Middle State Schools in Delaware, District of Columbia, Maryland, Puerto Rico, Canal Zone, Virgin Islands and Overseas. Philadelphia, Pa. Middle State Assn. of Colleges and Schools, 1978.

Guide to Middle States Schools in New Jersey. Philadelphia, Pa., Middle States Assn. of Colleges and Schools, 1978.

Guide to Middle States Schools in New York. Philadelphia, Pa., Middle States Assn. of Colleges and Schools, 1978.

Guide to Middle States Schools in Pennsylvania. Philadelphia, Pa., Middle States Assn. of Colleges and Schools, 1978.
Guide books list special programs, test data, grades and rank, and post-secondary plans of students.

Lovejoy's Career and Vocational School Guide. Clarence E. Lovejoy, 5th. ed. New York, Simon & Schuster, 1978.
Directory of institutions training for job opportunities.

Musicians Guide. See: Cultural/Recreational.

The New York Times Guide to Suburban Public Schools. Long Island, Westchester, Rockland, Connecticut, New Jersey. Maeroff and Buder. New York, Quadrangle/The N.Y. Times Book Co., 1976.
Gives descriptions and statistical information on school districts.

Official Guide to Catholic Educational Institutions and Religious Communities in the United States. New York, Catholic Institutional Directory Co.

Annual. A directory of catholic universities, colleges, junior colleges, nursing schools, secondary boarding schools, and religious orders for men and women in the U.S. Includes information on admission requirements, courses offered, facilities, costs.

Patterson's American Education. Mount Prospect, Il., Education Directories.

Annual. A comprehensive list of public and private schools, colleges, universities and other special schools in two main parts: school systems, arranged by states then by towns; directory of schools, colleges and universities classified by specialty. Includes officers of state, county and city educational systems, etc. and a list of educational associations.

Private Independent Schools. Wallingford, Conn., Bunting.

Annual. Gives fairly lengthy descriptions of a large selection of private schools and brief listings of others. Includes a list of educational associations.

Registry of Private Schools for Children with Special Educational Needs. See: Handicapped.

Employment Information

Ad Search: The National Want Ad. Newspaper. Milwaukee, Wi., Leibherr.

Weekly. Photocopies of want ads from 67 major U.S. newspapers.

College Placement Annual. Bethlehem, Pa., College Placement Council, Inc.

Annual. Lists occupational needs of corporate and government employers who recruit college graduates.

Digest of Executive Opportunities. New Canaan, Ct. General Executive Services Inc.

Weekly.

Directory of Private Employment Agencies. Washington, D.C., National Employment Association.

Federal Job Information Centers Directory. Washington, D.C., U.S. Civil Service Commission. G.P.O.

Finding a Job: A Resource for the Middle-Aged and Retired. Garden City, N.Y., Adelphi University Press, 1978.
> Lists state and non-profit employment agencies on a state basis.

Occupations in Demand at Job Services Offices. Washington, D.C., U.S. Department of Labor. Employment and Training Administration, U.S. Employment Service. G.P.O.
> Monthly bulletin. Identifies occupations for which large numbers of job openings were listed with public employment service computerized job banks during previous month.

Handicapped

Access Guide Directory. Rehabilitation International USA, 20 W 40th St. N.Y., 10018
> Annual. Directory of 275 handbooks to cities and transportation facilities throughout world. Free to disabled, handicapped and elderly persons.

The College Guide for Students with Disabilities. A Detailed Directory of Higher Education Services, Programs and Facilities Accessible to Handicapped Students in the U.S. Elinor Gollay, Cambridge, Ma., Abt Associates, 1976.
> Arranged geographically.

Directory of Agencies Serving the Visually Handicapped in the U.S. 20th. ed. New York, American Foundation for the Blind, 1978.

Directory of Facilities for Learning-Disabled and Handicapped. Careth Ellinson and James Cass. New York, Harper & Row, 1972.
> Includes "analytical descriptions of diagnostic facilities . . . , as well as descriptions of remedial, therapeutic and developmental programs." Listing is by states of the U.S. and the provinces of Canada. Index by names of institutions, and lists of facilities in major cities.

Directory for Exceptional Children. Boston, Ma., Porter Sargent Publications Inc., 1978.

> Gives information on public and private schools and treatment centers for the emotionally disturbed and socially maladjusted; psychiatric guidance clinics; facilities for orthopedic and neurological handicaps; facilities for the mentally retarded; schools for the blind, the partially sighted, the deaf and hard of hearing; speech and hearing clinics, etc. Includes list of associations, foundations and societies.

Public Welfare Directory: 1977–78. Michele Moore. Chicago, Il., American Public Welfare Association.

> Annual. Information concerning basic programs, practices and staff of all public welfare and related public agencies in the U.S. and Canada.

Registry of Private Schools for Children with Special Educational Needs. Baltimore, Md., National Educational Consultants, 1971.

> Arranged alphabetically by state. Index by type of disability served. Updating supplements are issued annually.

Health

American Dental Directory. Chicago, Il., American Dental Association.

> Annual. A geographical and alphabetical listing of dentists.

American Medical Directory. Littleton, Ma. PSG Publishing, 1979 5 v.

> A register of physicians of the U.S., Canal Zone, Puerto Rico, Virgin Islands, certain Pacific Islands, and U.S. physicians located temporarily in foreign countries, who possess a degree of Doctor of Medicine or Doctor of Osteopathy from an approved medical school. Arranged geographically.

Directory of Medical Specialists. Chicago, Il., Marquis Who's Who Inc.

> Annual. American Specialty Boards certified physicians.

Guide to Health Care Field. Chicago, Il., American Hospital Association.

> Annual. Central source of information on health care institutions, medical organizations, agencies, educational programs in the health field.

Handbook and Directory of Nursing Homes and Other Facilities for the Aged Within a 50-mile Radius of New York City. Eckman and Furman. New York, Basic Books Inc., 1975.

National Dirctory of Private Social Agencies. Queens Village, N.Y., Croner.

> Loose-leaf, up-dated monthly. Has subject and geographical listing.

U.S. Guide to Nursing Homes. Dan Greenberg. New York, Grosset & Dunlap, 1973.

> East, West and Midwest editions. By state, then city. Includes points to consider in choosing a home.

Moving and Home Purchase

Condominiums; How To Buy, Sell, and Live in Them. Genevieve Gray. New York, Barnes and Noble Books, 1976.

> Legal, financial and other aspects of condominium ownership.

Do-It-Yourself Moving. George Sullivan. New York, Macmillan, 1973.

The Fannie Mae Guide To Buying, Financing and Selling Your Home. Curt Tucker. Garden City, N.Y., Doubleday, 1978.

> Covers financing, housing market, law etc. for houses, condominiums, and co-operatives.

How To Move Your Family Successfully. Tucson, Az., H.P. Books, 1979.

Home for Sale by Owner. Gerald M. Steiner. Chicago, Ill., Ana-Doug Publishing, 1976.

> Legal and financial information and practical tips on home selling.

Religion

American Jewish Organization Directory. Margaret F. Goldstein, ed. 10th. ed. New York, Frenkel Mailing Service, 1978.
> Lists Jewish organizations, schools, synagogues and Israeli institutions in the U.S. and Canada.

Jewish Travel Guide. Sidney Lightman, ed Jewish Chronicle Publications, 25 Furnival St., London, England. No American Distributors, European Publisher's Representatives, Inc. and British Publications, Inc., 11-03 46th. Ave., Long Island City, New York, 11101.
> Lists organizations and synagogues in U.S. as well as Great Britain and Israel. U.S. section less complete than American Jewish Organization Directory.

The Official Catholic Directory. New York, P. J. Kenedy & Sons.
> Annual. Lists Archdioceses and clergy in U.S., territories and overseas missions. Arranged alphabetically by diocese and clergy. Parishes, missions and parochial schools within diocese.

Note: Most Protestant denominations have their own directories. A sample is included. Consult your minister for the directory for your church if it is not included on this list.

Directory of Churches—Conservative Baptist Association of America. Wheaton, Ill., Conservative Baptist Association of America.
> Annual. Geographically arranged directory.

Directory Unitarian Universalist Association. Boston, Ma., Unitarian Universalist Association.
> Annual. Geographically arranged directory.

The Episcopal Church Annual Including the Polish National Catholic Church of America and Canada. New York, Morehouse-Barlow Co.
> Annual. Alphabetical list of dioceses and churches within diocese.

Mennonite Yearbook. Scottdale, Pa., Mennonite Publishing House.

> Annual. Regional directory.

Year Book and Directory of the Christian Church. (Disciples of Christ) Indianapolis, Ind., The Christian Church.

> Annual. Geographically arranged directory.

Yearbook Lutheran Church of America. Philadelphia, Pa., Board of Publications of the Lutheran Church of America.

> Annual. Geography Directory of churches.

Yearbook United Church of Christ. New York., United Church of Christ.

> Annual. Geographical Directory of churches.

Retirement

National Directory of Retirement Residences: Best Places To Live When You Retire. Noverre Musson. Rev. ed., New York, Fell, 1973.

> State by state directory. Factors to consider in choosing.

Sunbelt Retirement: The Complete State-by-State Guide to Retiring in the South and the West of the U.S. New York, E. P. Dutton, 1978.

> Summarizes climate, cost of housing, food and cultural advantages by state with brief description of major cities.

Woodall's 1978 Retirement Communities Directory. New York, Grosset and Dunlop, 1978.

Guide to Retirement Living. Paul Holter. Chicago, Rand McNally & Co. 1973.

> Lists retirement communities, condominiums, apartments and trailer parks.

Where To Retire on a Small Income. Norman D. Ford, Greenlawn, N.Y., Harian, 1978.